D1206164

The Outdoor Handbook

Hamlyn
London · New York · Sydney · Toronto

Acknowledgements

Illustrations by Robin Anderson, Richard Corfield, Henry Fox, Stuart Perry, Michael Youens.
A number of the illustrations in this book originally appeared in Hamlyn all-colour paperbacks.

Colour plates
Animal Graphics 145 T, 145BR; Australian News and Information Bureau 47; Peter Baker 83, 95, 162; Barnaby's Picture Library 58, 168–169; Blacks of Greenock front jacket, top left, 35, 49T, 68–69, 85; Camera Press front jacket, bottom right; D. Church 19, 28, 54, 57, 66, 67, 92, 96; Cochrane's of Oxford 187; Bruce Coleman Ltd 163, 197; Colorsport 129, 138; D. Cummings 199 T + B, 200; W. F. Davidson 172; P. Eagar 117; Ford Photo Unit 167; Hamlyn Group Picture Library front jacket, top right, 72, 145B, 155, 159, 160, 175, 176; D. J. Murphy (Publishers) Ltd 157; T. Parker 24, 27, 33, 52, 53, 56, 59, 60, 61, 63, 64–65, 70–71, 82, 100, 194; B. Porteous 74, 79, 81; Raleigh Cycle Co. Ltd 190; A. Sidey 2–3; G. Shearn 46, 92, 97, 201T; Sport and General Press Agency 113, 114L, 118 T + BL, 126, 128, 130, 143; Tony Stone Associates back jacket; Swiss National Tourist Office 49B, 191T; Syndication International front jacket, bottom left, 6–7, 114R, 115, 118BR, 119, 121, 122, 124, 127, 135, 136, 140, 141; Youth Hostels Association 50 T + B; Diana Wyllie Ltd 192, 192–193, 195, 198, 201B.

Black and white illustrations
R. English 191B; Girl Guides Association 93; Scout Association 16–17 (I. Gibb), 34 (K. Oultram), 55, 195T; Youth Hostels Association 51 (C. Richards).

Published 1978 by
The Hamlyn Publishing Group Limited
London · New York · Sydney · Toronto
Astronaut House, Feltham, Middlesex, England
© Copyright The Hamlyn Publishing Group Limited 1978

All rights reserved. No part of this publication may be reproduced, stored in a retrieval system, or transmitted, in any form or by any means, electronic, mechanical, photocopying, recording or otherwise, without the permission of The Hamlyn Publishing Group Limited.

ISBN 0 600 36743 6

Printed in Great Britain

Contents

Introduction

Young people today have a more exciting choice of outdoor activities than ever before and this book has been specially created to help you enjoy a wide range of these.

The best-known and most popular sporting activities, such as soccer and skating, are described and also some of those less well-known, such as archery and kite flying. You can learn how to make a barbecue, hammock or kites, how to look after camping equipment or a bicycle and the best way to pack a rucksack. For those who like beachcombing there are suggestions for what to do with finds such as shells and attractively coloured pebbles. Those keen to take up riding will find a section on this subject to get them started.

With this enjoyment must come responsibility. Here, too, readers will find the encouragement they need to take care of the countryside, the plants and animals; how to recognise some of those they will most often see; how to behave for their own and other people's safety, and how to deal with accidents.

Because weather and terrain are so important in outdoor activities, there are sections on these subjects.

Each section is packed with full colour illustrations and diagrams so that every point is clearly made. So read the book and put all its hints and guidance into practice and have fun outdoors!

Map Reading & Navigation

A map is a passport to new places. It can take you up the road, just over the hill, or across the world, and you won't have to move a step! A map can tell you what a place looks like, whether it is hilly or flat, and where the rivers and creeks are; it can tell you where the people live, and how they move around on roads, paths and railways. You can learn about the history of a town from a map, you can discover why it was established where it is, and perhaps how it got its name; you can find out how the town grew from a small village, what the people do there, and how the town might grow into a city.

In this chapter we start to learn how to read a topographic map, how to extract some of the detail and information recorded there. We shall learn about the symbols used to mark features on the map, how to measure distances, and how to recognise hills and valleys. Then we shall see how we can use a compass, with the map, to find our position and how to get where we wish to go.

This chapter is just a start, a first step into a new world. If you want to learn more, you should look for books on map reading in the Geography section of your library, or ask the Librarian to look for you.

All the topics we shall discuss in

Conventional signs

	Main road		Marsh
	Secondary road		Cliff
	Minor road		Wood
	Track		Orchard
	Unfenced track		Church with tower
	Path		Church with spire
	Railway		Triangulation pillar
	Bridge	100	Contours at 20m intervals
	Level crossing	·148	Spot heights
	Cutting	P	Post office
	Embankment	PH	Public house
		T	Telephone call box

8

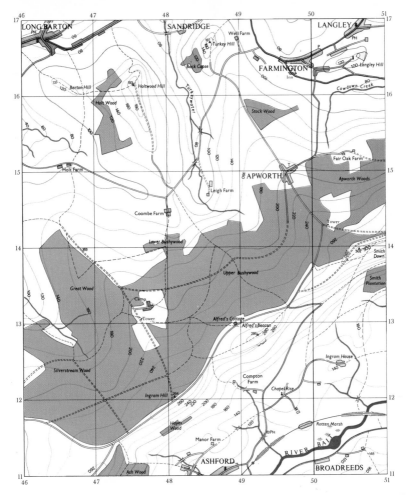

Scale 1:50 000   2 centimetres to 1 kilometre (one grid square)

1 kilometre = 0·6214 mile   1 mile = 1·6093 kilometres

the next pages make use of examples from the map on page 9. This is only a small map, and it may not look exactly like your local maps. You should get a map of your own area and work examples on that.

You can often obtain topographic maps from a local bookshop or stationer. In some places, such maps are harder to find. You could try a store which sells equipment for climbing, hiking or camping, or you could contact your local Scout or Girl Guide association.

Take your map with you when you go out. Compare it with the ground as you go, and follow your route on the map. Remember, a map is a friend, so get to know it well; it will tell you many things about the country around you.

Scale and distance

Scale has the meaning of ratio or proportion. The scale of a map is

Measuring distance along a road.

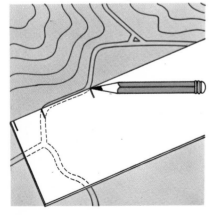

the comparison between a distance measured between two points on the map and the actual distance between the same two points on the ground.

There are three common ways of giving the scale on a map, all of which are shown on page 9: in words (two centimetres to one kilometre); as a *Representative Fraction*, or R.F. (1/50 000); or by a scale line. The scale line is marked into primary divisions to the right of the zero (kilometres and miles in the diagram), with secondary divisions to the left of the zero (100 metres and tenths of miles). The smaller the denominator in the R.F., the larger the scale of the map and the greater the detail that can be shown.

Straight-line distances between points on the map can be measured using a ruler or a pair of dividers. The map distance can then be compared with the scale line to obtain the distance on the ground. The R.F. can also be used to convert map measurement to ground measurement. For example, the distance between the churches at Langley Hill and Chapel Rise is 9·2 cm on the map, and the R.F. is 1/50 000; then the ground distance is 9·2 × 50 000 cm, or 4·6 km.

Distances along a winding path or road or river must be divided into a series of straight lines from bend to bend. The best way is to mark each straight section along the edge of a piece of stiff paper; at the end of each section, rotate the paper on the point of a pencil (to prevent the paper moving about) to the next section. When all sections have been measured, the distance can be obtained by comparing the paper with the scale line. For example, the distance along the road from the crossroads at Apworth to Alfred's Cottage is 2·8 km. This method is accurate over short distances, but over longer distances errors will be introduced because not all bends in paths and rivers can be shown on the map.

Symbols

Many important features cannot be shown clearly and to scale on a map. For example, if roads were drawn with their widths to scale, they would be too narrow to be seen easily on the map. The mapmaker uses a set of special symbols, or *conventional signs*, to represent such features. He may also use different colours to make map reading easier. The diagram on page 8 shows some common conventional signs; you should try to learn the symbols on your own map.

Grid references

Topographic maps of many countries are overprinted with a grid of one-kilometre squares. This grid provides an easy system for referring to any point on the map. The lines running up and down the map are *eastings*, and those running across

the map are *northings*. To refer to a one-kilometre square, give the number of the easting on the *left* of the square and the number of the northing *below* the square; always give the easting first. For example, the grid reference (G.R.) of the square containing Alfred's Beacon is 4912. To refer to a location more precisely, estimate tenths of kilometres within the square. For example, the reference to the triangulation pillar is found from:

Easting Line to west 49
        Tenths eastwards 2
Northing Line to south 12
        Tenths northwards 8

The full G.R. to the triangulation pillar is 492128 (see diagram below). This identifies a square 100 metres by 100 metres, to the east of easting 492, and to the north of northing 128. More examples from the map: The station at Ashford is at 491111. The church at Long Barton is at 462167.

A precise grid reference.

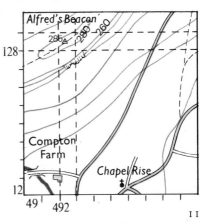

Relief

Maps are printed on flat paper, but the surface of the ground is not flat. Change in height from place to place is called *relief*. On most topographic maps relief is shown by *contour lines*. A contour line is a line on a map passing through all points with the same height above mean sea level. If you walk along a contour you follow a level path, and if you leave the contour you must go uphill or downhill. The distance between successive contour lines is the *vertical interval* (V.I.); in the map on page 9 the V.I. is 20 metres. Some maps show heights at points which have been accurately surveyed, usually at triangulation pillars or spot heights; they provide extra information about relief. There is a spot height at G.R. 468139.

Drawing a cross-section

Much can be learned about a piece of country by drawing a cross-section of it. The method is illustrated in the diagrams opposite, in which a cross-section from G.R. 466151 to G.R. 496149 is drawn. The first stage is to place a sheet of graph paper along the line of the section (figure a). Mark the crossing points of the contours, label them with their height, and note any other features such as rivers or roads. Next draw a base line equal to the length of the section (figure b). Choose a suitable vertical scale and mark heights corresponding to the contours crossing the section. Finally, join the points with a smooth line to obtain the cross-section (figure c), and show the special features. This method exaggerates the relief, because the horizontal and vertical scales are different; one centimetre corresponds to 50,000 cm horizontally, and to only 33 metres or 3,300 cm vertically. The *vertical exaggeration* is $50,000 \div 3,300$, or $15 \cdot 1$. Note that the closest contours correspond to the steepest slope.

Intervisibility

It is often of practical value to know if one point on the ground can be seen from another. Section drawing can be used to discover whether two points are intervisible, and to show ground that cannot be seen (*dead ground*). An observer at Holt Farm could see clearly to Apworth, but figure c opposite shows that Leigh Farm and Turkey Water are in dead ground from this position. They are also in dead ground from an observer at Apworth, due to the convex slope of the hill. A series of cross-sections can be drawn to show an observer's view in all directions from a hilltop.

The application of section drawing and calculations of intervisibility ('line-of-sight') will become clearer if you take your map to a hilltop and see which features are visible, and which are in dead ground. Draw

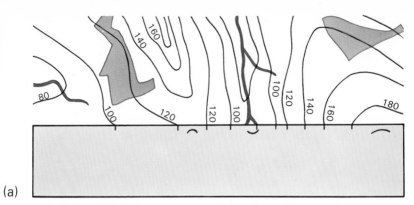

(a)

Drawing a cross-section.

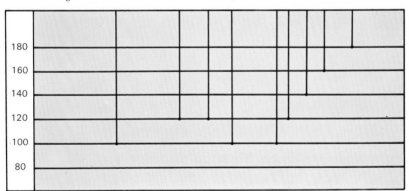

(b)

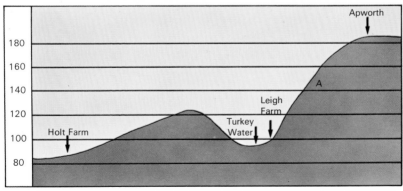

(c)

An ordnance survey map shows you at a glance what the terrain is like.

sections from your position on the hilltop, and identify features which are restricting your view. Compare your section drawing carefully with the ground before you, and see how well you have predicted the view.

Landforms

It is very important to be able to build up in your mind a three-dimensional view of the area shown on the map. Illustrated opposite are some of the common features and the patterns of contours which might represent them on a map. Find examples in the map on page 9.

(a) *Spur:* a projection of high ground into lower ground.
Valley: a long narrow depression between higher ground.

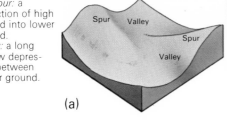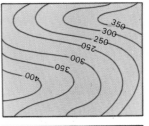

(b) *Ridge:* a long narrow stretch of high ground.
Col, or *saddle:* a depression or pass in a line of hills or between two summits.

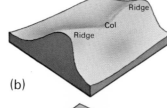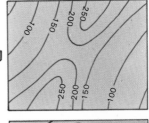

(c) *Plateau:* a long flat block or 'table' of high ground.

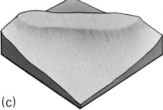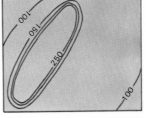

(d) *Escarpment:* a ridge with a steep scarp slope on one side and a more gentle dip slope or back slope on the other. The highest part is the crest.

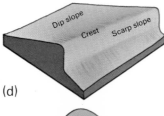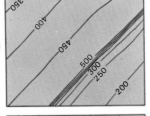

(e) *Knoll:* a small rounded hill.

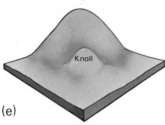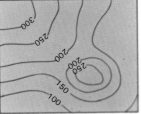

Direction

The *bearing* of an object refers to its direction from an observer with respect to a fixed line running north–south through the observer's position. The bearing is measured clockwise from the north to the object, so the bearings of A and B in the figure below are 120° and 270°.

Because the North Magnetic Pole

similar to that shown below, showing the angle between true north

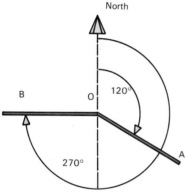

North points

Measuring bearings

is not located at the North Geographic Pole, the line pointing to *magnetic north* is different from that pointing to geographic or *true north*, and the bearing measured from these lines will be different. They are called *magnetic bearings* and *true bearings* respectively. In addition, *grid north* is different from both magnetic and true north, so the *grid bearing* is different from both the magnetic and true bearings. Most topographic maps have a diagram

and magnetic north (called the *magnetic variation*) and the angle between true north and grid north.

To measure a grid bearing, draw a thin pencil line from the observer

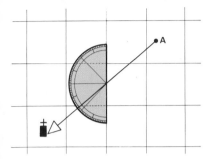

Measuring a grid bearing

to the object, and measure the angle between this line and a north–south grid line (an easting) with a protractor (diagram below left). Don't forget to measure clockwise from the north.

As an aid to converting from one kind of bearing to another, draw for your own map a diagram like that shown below. This will help you to remember what angles to add or subtract to convert bearings. (Be careful when you draw your diagram, because the angles are different in different places, and may be to the east or west of true north.) For our map, the grid bearing of G.R. 492128 from G.R. 506139 is 231°, so its true bearing is 232°, and its magnetic bearing is 240°; the magnetic bearing of G.R. 505164 from G.R. 485167 is 105°, so its true bearing is 97° and its grid bearing is 96°. (Check this yourself on the map.)

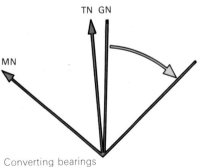

Converting bearings

A group of Scouts use an ordnance survey map to plan their route before setting out on a walk.

Finding north

An important part of using a map is the ability to locate the position on the map corresponding to your position on the ground. We shall look at this in detail later, but a first step is to *set the map*, that is, to align north on the map with north in the actual country. There are several ways of finding north.

1 By compass. The compass needle points to magnetic north. Lay the map flat on the ground, and place the compass on the map with its axis (the $0°$–$180°$ line) on the magnetic north–south line. Then gently rotate the map until the magnetic north–south line coincides with the compass needle.

2 By the sun. If the sun is visible, an approximate north–south line can be found using a watch. In the northern hemisphere, hold the watch face upwards in a horizontal position, and turn it until the hour hand points towards the sun; then the line bisecting the angle between the hour hand and a line joining the centre of the dial to 12 o'clock points to south (diagram below left). In the southern hemisphere, if a line joining the centre of the dial to 12 o'clock is pointed at the sun, the line bisecting the angle between this line and the hour hand points to north (diagram below). Do not forget to adjust for 'summer time' or 'daylight saving time'. If the sun is obscured by clouds, it may nevertheless cast a shadow. Hold a pencil upright on the map; the shadow points away from the sun.

3 By comparing the map with features on the ground. Align the map so that an easily identifiable straight length of feature on the map is parallel with the same feature on the ground; suitable features might be a railway or road, a length of river, or the crest of an escarpment. North can be determined from the north point on the map.

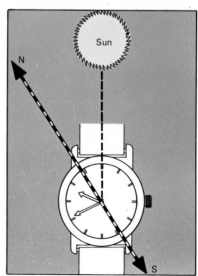

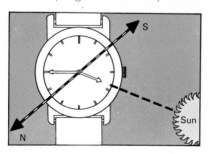

The Silva compass

The Silva compass is light, easy to use, and inexpensive. It has a direction line, a magnetic needle and a scale of degrees. To take a bearing to an object, stand squarely facing the object, holding the compass in front of you in one hand, and point the direction line at the object (diagram *b* below). Turn the scale with your other hand, so that the compass needle points to zero. The magnetic bearing can be read where the scale of degrees meets the direction line. Diagram *c* below shows a bearing of 50°. The Silva compass is widely used in orienteering.

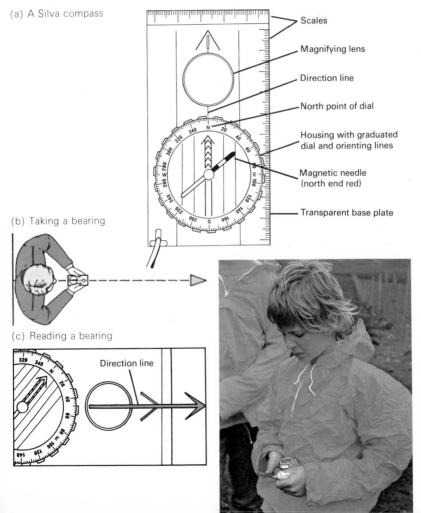

(a) A Silva compass

Scales

Magnifying lens

Direction line

North point of dial

Housing with graduated dial and orienting lines

Magnetic needle (north end red)

Transparent base plate

(b) Taking a bearing

(c) Reading a bearing

Direction line

Finding position

Plane-table method

Fix the map to a plane-table or other flat surface such as a map-board, and set the map as accurately as possible (see page 18). Choose three objects in the country which you can identify on the map; if possible, they should be 120° apart. Draw lines from the objects in the country through their counterparts on the map and towards yourself (diagram *a* below). If they intersect in a point, this is your position. In practice, it is more likely that they will form a *triangle of error* (diagram *b*), in which your true position lies.

Compass method

Choose three objects in the country which you can identify on the map, 120° apart if possible, and take compass bearings to them. Convert the magnetic compass bearings to grid bearings (see page 17). Now find the *backbearings*, that is, the bearings from the objects back to your position; to obtain backbearings, add 180° to bearings less than 180°, and subtract 180° from bearings greater than 180°. (For example, from G.R. 492128 the grid bearings to G.R.

Diagrams (a) and (b) below show the plane-table method for finding your position on a map. Diagram (c) shows the compass method, for which you must learn how to find backbearings.

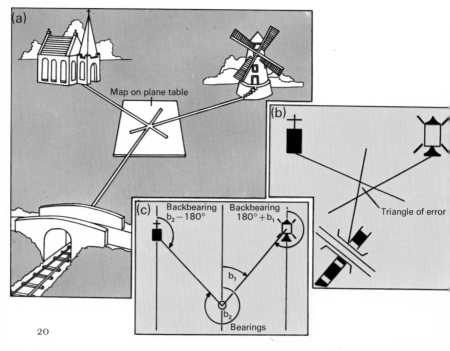

476130 and G.R. 506139 are 278° and 51°; the corresponding back-bearings are 98° and 231°. (See diagram *c* on page 20.)

From each object, draw a line along the backbearing. These lines should all pass through your position, and so should intersect in a point, but again it is likely that there will be a triangle of error. This method of finding position is called *resection*. For detailed location within the triangle of error, we must look more closely at the relationship between map and ground.

Relating map to ground

In relating map to ground, we need to use our knowledge about landforms from pages 14 and 15, and to apply it to smaller and less distinct features. The best way to learn to do this successfully is to practise on the ground with your own map, and to look for some of the things which the map does not show explicitly but only indicates. For example, there is likely to be a small knoll at G.R. 486114 (compare the contours with those in figure *e* on page 15), and there may be another at Chapel Rise (G.R. 495120); though small, these features should be easily recognisable. The illustration below shows square 4811 on a larger scale, that is, 1/25,000, with a smaller vertical interval; now the terrain features can be seen more clearly.

A larger scale of map with a smaller vertical interval will give a clearer picture of the terrain features of an area. The illustration shows (left) square 4811 at a scale of 1:50,000 and (right) the same area at the larger scale of 1:25,000. Now you can see clearly that Manor Farm is situated on a knoll.

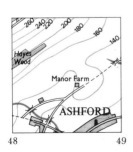

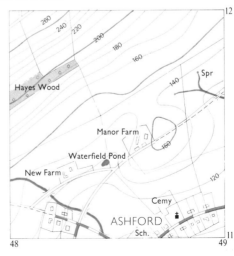

Walking a route

When you are using a map to plan a hike, you will usually pick out some prominent features to use as bounds and landmarks, and you will walk from one landmark to the next. You will need to measure distances and bearings from the map, and it is best to do this before you set out.

(Don't forget to convert grid bearings to magnetic bearings.)

You should make an estimate of the time it will take you to walk the route you have chosen. To do this you need to know how fast you walk in different kinds of country. Use a table like that shown below to record the time you take to walk one kilometre over different ground.

	Grass	Light vegetation	Heavy vegetation
Downhill			
Level			
Uphill			

Scouts learn how to use the Silva compass with the aid of a demonstration model.

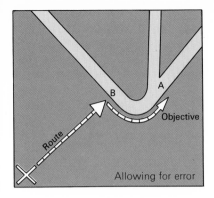

Allowing for error

It is easy to make small errors of a few degrees when walking over rough ground. If you might miss one of your bounds unless you are extremely accurate, you could allow for error by heading for a more easily recognisable feature. For example, in the diagram above, if you were to walk towards the track junction A, a small error to the south could make you miss it; however, if you aim for the track at B, and then walk south to A, you are less likely to become lost.

The illustration below shows how you can avoid an obstacle without losing your route. If you come to an obstacle (A), change direction by 90°, and walk until you are clear of it (B); count the number of paces you take. Now return to your original bearing until you are on the other side of the obstacle (C), change direction by 90°, and walk the same number of paces back to your original route (D).

You will find more on walking in the chapters on Hiking and Orienteering.

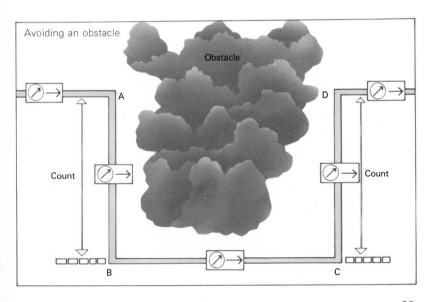

Avoiding an obstacle

Outdoor Safety & Survival

Minor emergencies of one kind or another occur all the time in outdoor activities; they tend to be trivial and easily forgotten. The really big emergency may never arise in years, but the outdoor enthusiast must be ready if one does suddenly loom up. It may be a rolling, low bank of cloud enveloping the trail ahead, or the sudden onset of cold, dank freezing mist; it could be a swirling, blinding whiplash of rain, with hailstones or sleet to follow; or sea fret may blow in from the sea on a morning that seemed calm and sunny. Plans, however well made, quickly tend to go wrong as hikers find themselves struggling with cold, very wet clothing and sodden kit.

Survival means being prepared for all possible emergencies outdoors. Team work and morale are the factors needed to ensure survival; team work means that the leader has 100 per cent support.

The sudden onset of mist is a hazard that walkers in the hills may have to face, so, unlike this walker in the Lake District, never set out alone or in pairs.

Adder

In open country you should always be on the lookout for snakes. Europe's only poisonous snake is the adder, which lives mainly in moorlands and clearings or the edges of woodlands and forested areas.

Grass snake

Smooth snake

Know your snakes!

Outdoor safety covers much more than the hazards of weather in rough, hilly country or mountains; in boating and canoeing, for example, your safety depends on your skills, and skills are needed to avoid getting lost on backpacking treks and bush walks. There are hazards underfoot, too, such as snakes! In Europe, the adder is the only poisonous snake: fortunately, only seven deaths were recorded in the first half of this century in Britain. The male is dull cream, yellow, grey or pale green with black markings, while the female is red, brown or gold with red or brown markings. Both are about 55 to 60 cm in length. The dark zig-zag line down the back with spots either side easily distinguishes adders from the harmless grass or smooth snakes. Adders hibernate in 'dens', rocky crevices or holes used year after year, in winter; forty or more adders huddle together for warmth, coiled and looped around each other, about 30 cm below ground in Britain and 120 cm or more in Scandinavia.

The grass snake is much larger than the adder; in Britain, females average 120 cm or more in length, males somewhat less, but in southern Europe they are much larger still. All are a beautiful olive green colour. The smooth snake is quite

25

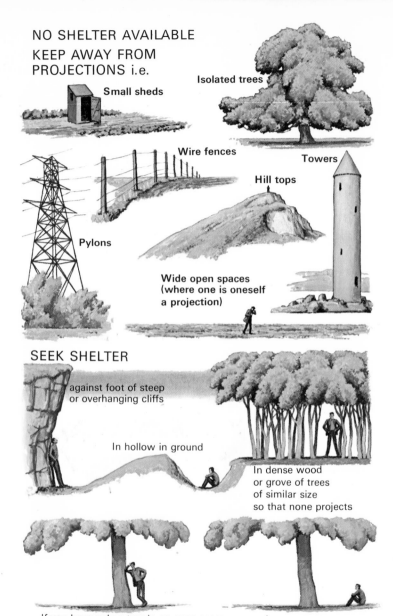

NO SHELTER AVAILABLE
KEEP AWAY FROM PROJECTIONS i.e.

Small sheds

Isolated trees

Wire fences

Towers

Hill tops

Pylons

Wide open spaces (where one is oneself a projection)

SEEK SHELTER

against foot of steep or overhanging cliffs

In hollow in ground

In dense wood or grove of trees of similar size so that none projects

If you have only a tree in an open space ·
DO NOT lean against it but keep several feet away and **do not touch it**

Improvise anything to make emergency shelters in bad weather, such as upturned boats on beaches or by lakes.

rare; it is roughly the size of an adder and grey-brown.

Watch out for sluggish adders when hiking or camping in the spring, when they sun themselves on warm stones. August and September, when the young are born, are times when adders frequent damp, rough country near the sea.

Campers and bushwalkers in Australia need to watch for the poisonous elapine snakes, which are one of the five families of snakes known there; of the 130 species of snakes in Australia, 70 belong to the elapine family, so beware!

Sheltering in bad weather conditions

Thunderstorms frequently interrupt projects in the mountains in unsettled summer weather. If you are caught in the open, out of reach of any natural protection, lie flat on your stomach, face downwards, with a groundsheet or waterproof of some kind on top. This simple method was used successfully by Allied soldiers in World War II. Alternatively, sit down on the ground, with your knees bent up and your head and hands on your knees, looking like a rock! Avoid projections likely to attract lightning, especially lone trees, pylons, wire fences and towers.

If an emergency occurs, such as a badly sprained or broken ankle, an eye injury, unexpected illness, or exposure to severe cold, then survival until rescue is the main consideration. Get out of the wind, which can chill and even kill in the hills and mountains. In a desert, where shelter from great heat is needed, wind may keep heat at bay, and thus prove a friend.

Improvise and use anything at hand to make a shelter, such as an upturned boat on a wild and lonely beach. In the Lake District, sheep pens are walled; there are many fine stone walls in other parts of

Tents are best pitched by stone walls which offer protection from wind, rain or other bad weather.

Camping by the sea in Denmark; straw windbreaks protect tents from onshore breezes.

England and in Scotland and Wales. Pitch tents to take full advantage of such walls. If tents are not being carried, then improvise a lean-to shelter against a wall with a groundsheet, as cyclists do to protect their cycles at night when camping. Whatever the hazard – wind, rain, snow, sleet or sun – there will be some way to tackle it using common sense and initiative.

Hurdles, such as wattle (made with osiers, which are young willows) and chestnut, make splendid windbreaks. Farmers use them widely in fields at lambing time;

In an emergency, sheltered hollows can be dug in snow.

forestry schemes make use of them to hold marram grass and young trees in place on sandy slopes. In Denmark, hinged windbreaks are used to shield tents against strong breezes. Survival may mean digging a shelter away from a gale force wind in the side of a golf bunker; shallow hollows against driving snow are better than nothing, so long as energy is conserved. If the light is fading and time is against building adequate shelter, make the very most of rocks, shrubs, scrub trees, anything at hand. Lean-tos make the best temporary bivouacs or shelters.

Sending distress signals

When temporary shelter has been achieved, then every effort must be made to make your position known as soon as possible. This can only be done by signals. It is unlikely that radio will be available for use by a hiking party caught by a snow blizzard on a windswept fell, or by youth hostellers enveloped by sudden low cloud on a dangerous, boggy moor. The most that can be expected is that the leader will have a small transistor for listening to weather bulletins, news and time signals for checking watches.

The risk of fire is taken very seriously in Britain and many other countries. Fire wardens are alert for any sign of smoke or fire in plantations of young trees, on gorse-covered hills and wide expanses of

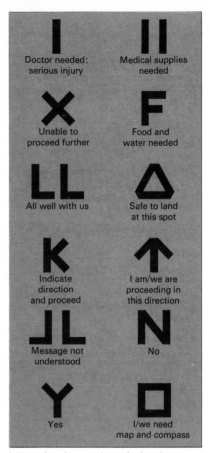

International ground-to-air signals are easily seen by low-flying helicopters or aircraft. Use stones, clumps of weeds, clothing or equipment.

commons, mountain heaths and grazing areas. Smoke signals by day and fire signals by night are therefore sure to be seen. Ground-to-air signals can be made in many ways to attract attention. They can be made boldly in snow or sand, ensuring that the essential outline of the signals is maintained. Page 29 depicts the recognized ground-to-air signals. Stones and branches of trees may be used, or else clothing, equipment, pieces of slate, clumps of weeds with soil, in fact, almost anything. A low-flying helicopter or aircraft can see ground-to-air signals more clearly than most ground watchers realise.

In daytime, three fires equally spaced apart and giving plenty of smoke are a recognised distress signal in many parts of the world. Smoke is produced by placing anything wet on the fire, such as handfuls of wet green leaves, bracken, heather, weeds or almost any kind of wet rag; trees should only be stripped if nothing else is available. Great care must be taken in making fires of any kind in situations where wood is plentiful, especially if it is

Morse code

A .—	S ...		
B —...	T —		
C —.—.	U ..—	**Ways to memorise morse**	
D —..	V ...—	Dots	Dashes
E .	W .——	. E	— T
F ..—.	X —..—	.. I	—— M
G ——.	Y —.——	... S	——— O
H	Z ——..	.... H	(no four dashes)
I ..	1 .————	 5	————— Zero
J .———	2 ..———		
K —.—	3 ...——	Opposites	
L .—..	4 ....—	A .—	N —.
M ——	5	U ..—	D —..
N —.	6 —....	R .—.	K —.—
O ———	7 ——...	V ...—	B —...
P .——.	8 ———..	W .——	G ——.
Q ——.—	9 ————.	F ..—.	L .—..
R .—.	0 —————	P .——.	X —..—

'Odd men out'

C —.—.
J .———
Q ——.—
Y —.——
Z ——..

•—•—•—•—• To attract attention 'Hey!' 'Hi!' etc.

•—• End of message 'Roger' (R)

•••———••• 'Help!' signal SOS (repeated)

When using a flag to send morse, wave it to your left for a dash and to your right for a dot. Make sure that the flag contrasts with your surroundings.

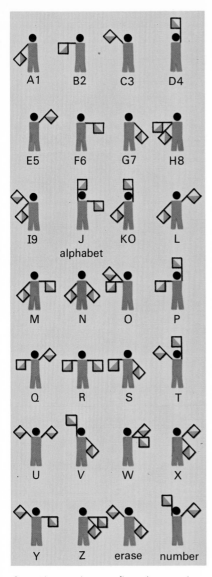

A1   B2   C3   D4

E5   F6   G7   H8

I9   J   KO   L
alphabet

M   N   O   P

Q   R   S   T

U   V   W   X

Y   Z   erase   number

Semaphore, using two flags, is a good way of sending distress signals during daylight.

breezy. At night only one fire is necessary for warmth, to keep up morale and to attract attention.

Steel mirrors can be used with great success for signalling in daytime; their advantage is that they can be used in mountains, hills, deserts, bush, wide areas of fells, commons, estuaries and similar situations. A polished tin lid is a good substitute, or a small handbag mirror. The scope is limited since direct rays of sunlight are needed to get a good flash; it is also essential to sweep the horizon continuously once you have been successful in obtaining a flash. In the United States and Canada steel mirrors from toilet bags have proved very successful in emergencies on large lakes and at sea. It is important to realise that aircraft can pick up mirror signals on hazy days with the sun hardly visible, even though ground signallers cannot see the plane. Keep signals going continuously.

In emergency, an item of clothing can be used as a flag signal on any kind of pole attached to a tree, especially if there is a good breeze blowing. The colour of the 'flag'

Lantern and torch useful for signalling.

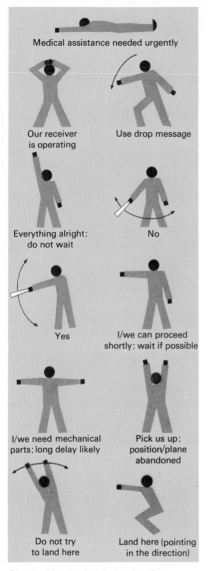

Our receiver
is operating

Use drop message

Everything alright;
do not wait

No

Yes

I/we can proceed
shortly; wait if possible

I/we need mechanical
parts; long delay likely

Pick us up;
position/plane
abandoned

Do not try
to land here

Land here (pointing
in the direction)

Standard body signals to aircraft can be used if your position is located by an air rescue team.

must contrast with the basic colour of the surrounding vegetation. Such 'flags' have been effective in Australian bushwalking emergencies. American Scouts carry an approved lightweight rescue blanket on outdoor projects in wild country which has one side coloured orange, ideal for contrast on snow, and the other side coloured silver for use on grass, sand or earth. Either side can be picked up by radar. These blankets have attracted much attention at international camps as they are excellent for use in so many countries.

The use of the morse code is accepted all over the world in emergency. Signals can be sent by torch, flashlight or lantern at night, and by whistle, car horn, mirror, buzzer and other devices, or by using a flag. The international distress call SOS sent by morse has saved a great many lives in outdoor emergencies. Survival could depend on a knowledge of morse code.

Semaphore, using two flags, is another method of sending signals that is well worth knowing for use during daylight.

Another means of signalling often used in mountain search and rescue operations are flares. A standard form of use has been agreed: *red* flares are used to indicate the 'position of the accident' or 'I require aid'; *white* flares are used to acknowledge messages; *green* flares are used to recall to base. A succession of notes on a whistle or bell may also be used to recall to base.

Once a party has been located, standard body signals to aircraft can be used and these save valuable time. Do not over-dramatise them. It is essential for sound survival that you keep calm when located for rescue.

Survival equipment

Campers use boulders to keep tents securely pitched on a cold and snowy site in Glencoe, Argyll.

Survival equipment is best kept by the party leader in a lightweight waterproof bag with drawcord top. (Bags sold for covering theodolites during outdoor survey work in rain are ideal.) The emergency whistle needs to be kept free of fluff and dust; the mirror must be well polished at all times and matches should be kept in a waterproof tin or box. The morse flag in light-

A large polythene bag with air holes cut in it makes an emergency bivouac. Use a rucksack to keep legs and hands warm and do not sit directly on the ground.

weight material folds very small; the stick should always be improvised, never carried as part of the equipment. Keep a daily check on torches, batteries and bulbs, for lives may depend on them working efficiently. If preferred, all matches can be waterproofed by dipping their heads in melted wax or candle grease; shredded candle ends make excellent firelighters in damp places.

There are many ways of making a fire. In Australia, bushwalkers carry hand lenses round their necks on cords so that the sun easily provides fire when needed. American backpackers carry some steel wool, such as a scouring pad that is not impregnated with soap. They hold the two live cells from a flashlight in one hand, with the cells making firm contact. The steel wool is then shredded out a little and one end is tucked under the bottom cell. The upper end of the pad is then placed in contact with the contact pole of the upper cell. It will soon glow well, enough to light some dry tinder and

33

start a fire on a wet morning. Great care must always be taken, however, as it is essential that fire is produced only where it is needed and can be controlled.

Remember that survival often depends on initiative. If no hand lens is carried then in an emergency a camera lens or binoculars lens would provide a focus at high noon in sun. Even clear ice has been shaped into a convex lens to provide fire.

Survival projects

The Great Adventure Hike at the 14th World Scout Jamboree in Norway in 1975 showed what can be done by young people today; no less

Members of a Scout patrol test their survival techniques on a hike in Norway.

than 12,000 of the 18,000 Scouts in camp, representing 98 countries between them, volunteered for the 24-hour test in the mountains of mid-Norway at a height over 1,000 metres. 1,500 patrols, each consisting of eight boys all unknown to one another, were selected by computer to ensure an international mix. The boys were allowed to choose from four categories of hike ranging from 10 km to 25 kms in tough, stony terrain at the limit of tree growth. The leaders were all Scandinavian boys; very many patrols had no common language between them! All patrols had specific projects to carry out; they lived on emergency rations plus whatever they could find in the mountains. They slept underneath black plastic sheets under the stars to ensure good conservation. There were no casualties and the patrols hardly saw each other throughout. As an experiment in survival technique it was a remarkable success.

I did the test myself, both in the mountains at just over 1000 metres, and later in another part of Norway, Telemark, with less stony conditions underfoot so that I could walk further. In the mid-Norway test I carried emergency rations including tinned kipper fillets, crispbreads, margarine, honey, glucose tablets, chocolate and dried fruit (apricots). I drank only water from mountain streams.

I collected some air-dried mutton and ham from a mountain hut; I found this satisfying but salty, and had to drink a large quantity of water with it. Growing on the large, flat stones in the mountains I found plenty of the grey lichen known as Alpine Ladies' Mantle; it grows only in pure unpolluted air. It tasted like crunchy, nutty breakfast cereal and was delicious. Survival on this is possible for a very long time. Freshwater shrimps abounded in the clear, cold streams if you could catch them, using handkerchiefs as nets. Berries grew everywhere in profusion. I stuck to the ones I knew, especially a sweet, full-flavoured bilberry. I used less than half of my emergency rations. Sleeping in a down bag, under a plastic sheet to offset dew, was easy once a comfortable spot sheltered from the wind had been found.

In Telemark a week later, the going was easier underfoot. Berries were even more profuse and delicious; I met Norwegians of all ages, some in their 70's, gathering them by the rucksack for winter preserves and meat garnishes. Fish was easier to find and catch. Sleeping was easier to arrange. It would be difficult to find a more beautiful, unspoiled and serene country than Norway in mid-summer.

Golden rules for survival

Finally, a few golden rules for survival in emergencies:

1 Keep calm; think the situation over carefully, make a plan and stick to it.

2 Conserve energy, food and water, if need be. Don't sing. Keep morale high. Talk safety and survival.

3 Keep as warm as possible, using everything available, especially glucose.

4 Watch for exhaustion and exposure signs.

5 Decide on the best way to attract attention in the circumstances. Act on this decision with discretion and skill.

6 Treat any accident as best you can. If in doubt, keep the patient warm; reassure constantly and never leave him/her alone.

Survival is certain. Rescue is only a matter of time. Always remember that.

The correct equipment and sound team work ensure survival for professional climbers such as these.

First Aid

Accidents will happen, particularly to young people enjoying themselves outdoors. A knowledge of first aid is invaluable at such times.

First of all, what is first aid? It is not treatment designed to make the doctor unnecessary. It is *first* aid, performed by a person on the spot to help the patient until such time as proper medical aid arrives. Its purpose is to relieve the patient of unnecessary fear and worry, to reduce his suffering, to prevent, if possible, his injury from worsening, and perhaps to begin his recovery. Speed is usually important, which means that it is no use trying to learn first aid when the accident has happened.

It is possible to learn *some* of the principles of first aid from this chapter, but the best way to learn is by joining a course. First aid courses are run by the Red Cross and other organisations. Your local telephone directory or perhaps your school teacher will help you to find your nearest branch.

Pulse and breathing rates

First aiders should know about pulse and breathing rates. The average pulse of a normal adult is between 60 and 80 per minute, a child's is somewhat higher. A shocked patient's pulse rate will be much higher. The best places to take the pulse are just above the wrist or in front of the ear. Find these places on yourself or friends and practise taking pulse rates. The breathing rate can be counted by watching the rise and fall of a person's chest. Normally it will be about 14 per minute at rest. Stress of any kind could increase it a lot.

Drowning

Serious accidents outdoors are often connected with water, so it is quite possible that a first aider will find himself coping with a case of drowning. If breathing has stopped, a method of artificial respiration must be practised.

Tilt the patient's head as far back as possible and seal your mouth over the patient's open mouth.

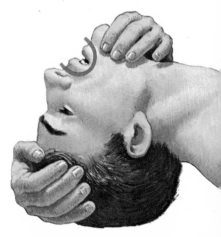

Artificial respiration

Mouth to Mouth Method

Speed is essential, and the following actions should not be performed deliberately one by one, but should become a smooth routine. Practice makes perfect, and on a first aid course, manikins (models) may be provided for practising.

A check for mouth-to-mouth respiration.

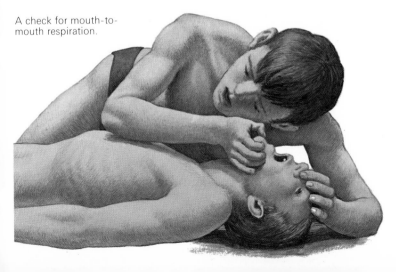

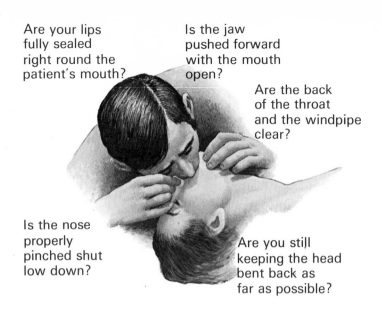

Are your lips fully sealed right round the patient's mouth?

Is the jaw pushed forward with the mouth open?

Are the back of the throat and the windpipe clear?

Is the nose properly pinched shut low down?

Are you still keeping the head bent back as far as possible?

Points to check in the mouth-to-mouth method of artificial respiration.

1 Turn the patient on his back.

2 Tilt his head back as far as possible, so that his nostrils are pointing upwards.

3 Pinch his nose shut with forefinger and thumb (see illustration).

4 Make sure the patient's mouth is open. If not, open it by pulling the jaw.

5 Clear his mouth. Stick in your forefinger and quickly run it round his mouth to make sure.

6 Take a deep breath and seal your mouth round the patient's.

7 Breathe steadily and firmly into the patient's mouth. If properly performed, the patient's chest will rise.

8 Remove your mouth and allow the patient's lungs to empty. You can feel with your face the breath coming out (see illustration).

9 Repeat stages 6, 7 and 8 until the doctor arrives and asks you to stop.

It follows from 9 that you should shout or send for help between breaths. The first five breaths given to the patient should be rapid, to replenish the oxygen in the patient's blood. Afterwards, the breaths should be firm, full and regular rather than fast.

The Holger Nielson Method

This is less effective than the mouth-to-mouth method of respiration, but may be an easier method for the novice to master.

1 As before, make sure that the

patient's mouth is absolutely clear.
2 Lay him on his stomach.
3 Turn his head to lay on his hands.
4 Kneel at his head and place your hands, with thumbs touching and fingers spread, as shown in illustration 1.

5 Rock forwards until your arms are upright. Do not push downwards – your body weight will be sufficient to drive the air from his lungs (illustration 2).
6 Rock backwards, sliding your hands along the patient's upper arm to near his elbows, allowing

The Holger Nielson method of artificial respiration.

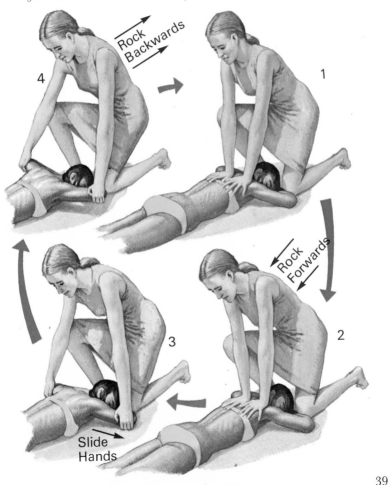

your backwards movement to lift his elbows slightly off the ground (illustrations 3 and 4).

7 Return your hands to the position in illustration 1 and repeat operations 5 and 6.

Aim at an unhurried, smooth routine.

Shock

Severe injury can cause shock – not the bewilderment or fright which an accident might naturally produce in a patient, but a serious condition which, if unchecked, is dangerous. Great loss of blood can cause it, or severe burning or fractures.

Recognition

The shocked patient will be pale or grey, cold yet sweating, probably breathing weakly yet very fast, and with a weak, fast pulse. Mentally he might seem distant, slow to understand. He might speak slowly. He is likely to ask for a drink, but must not be given one.

Prevention

Note the heading – 'prevention'. A patient displaying the above symptoms must be got to hospital at once. He is beyond the first aider, whose job is to *prevent* shock in a badly injured patient.

The first task is to stop any bleeding. This is discussed later. Secondly, make the patient rest. Insist he lies down. The illustration shows the best position. Loosen his clothing. Thirdly, keep him warm. Do not try to increase his temperature, just wrap him with blankets or coats so

Good and bad positions for the shocked patient.

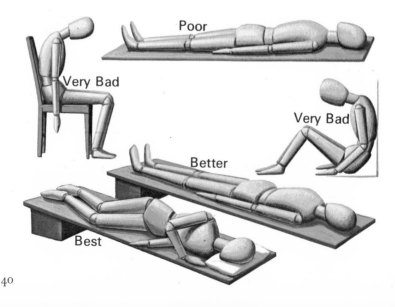

Poor

Very Bad

Very Bad

Better

Best

that he does not lose heat. Put coats beneath him if he is lying on the ground. Lastly, give him comfort and encouragement. Dress his wounds, talk to him quietly and sensibly. Let him know you can look after him. But do not fuss or let any onlookers fuss over him. And remember – allow no drinks. Anything in the mouth could choke him – especially if he becomes unconscious later.

Bleeding

Minor cuts and grazes, while benefitting from cleaning and dressing, will frequently heal themselves. This section deals with the action required for a bad wound causing severe bleeding. The first thing to do is to raise the bleeding part. Lay the patient down to raise a leg or to raise an arm in the air. However, do not do this if you suspect a fracture. Use your finger and thumb to close the wound and hold the edges together. Apply pressure and maintain it for 10 minutes to allow a clot to form. Press a pad of material over the wound and secure with a bandage. Improvise, if necessary, with handkerchiefs, scarves or material torn from clothing. Press the dressing well on to the wound, into it if necessary. Do not attempt a tourniquet unless you have professional supervision. Keep the injured limb still and raised, and if bleeding persists add further bandages – do not remove the original bandage. Check for shock.

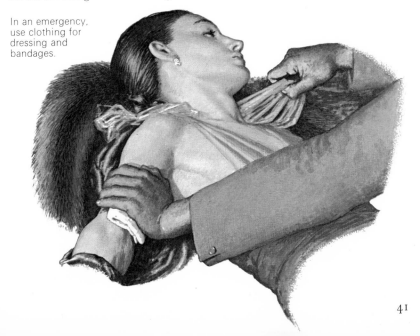

In an emergency, use clothing for dressing and bandages.

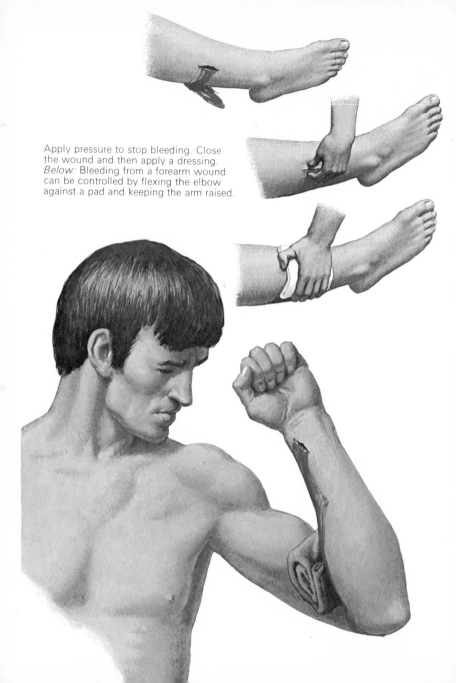

Apply pressure to stop bleeding. Close
the wound and then apply a dressing.
Below: Bleeding from a forearm wound
can be controlled by flexing the elbow
against a pad and keeping the arm raised.

Burns

If a victim's clothes are flaming, get him to the ground at once, and smother the flames by wrapping a blanket or coat round him. But be sensible – if clothes are only smouldering, rip them off and stamp out the fire.

The burn should be immersed in cold water immediately and kept there until the pain fades, which could take 15 minutes or more. Remember, the patient may suffer shock (see earlier). Remove tight clothing, as swelling may develop. Dress the burn with clean materials. If burnt material is sticking to the burn, do not attempt to remove it. Keep the burnt part raised, and get the patient to hospital.

Fractures and sprains

Where bones meet at joints, they are kept in position by ligaments. Ligaments may get torn; for example, if a foot is wrenched it may cause tearing of the ankle ligaments. This is known as a sprain. Mild sprains will cause a swelling, which can be immunised with a cold compress, that is, a cloth soaked in cold water, wrung out and wrapped round the sprained joint. When ligaments tear they may displace a bone; this is known as a dislocation. A fracture is when the bone actually breaks. A broken bone nearly always means that ligaments are torn, so you can see that sprains, dislocations and fractures are related, and often occur together.

It is difficult to be sure if a patient has suffered a fracture. If a blow is followed by a pain, suspect a fracture. The injured part may look to be bent, or otherwise strangely positioned. The patient may be unable to move it, or it may be swollen.

The first aider's general principles are to prevent movement of the injured part, control severe bleeding, if any, and keep the patient still. Bear in mind, too, that the patient may suffer from shock (see earlier).

An injured limb is secured against the patient's body, for example a broken leg is secured against the good one. Always move the broken limb as little as possible, and put padding between the broken limb

A collarbone fracture immobilised; the hand should be kept as high as possible.

43

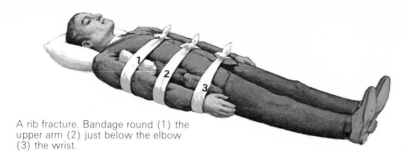

A rib fracture. Bandage round (1) the upper arm (2) just below the elbow (3) the wrist.

and the part to which it is secured. Materials for padding and slings must often be improvised, but it is amazing what can be done with socks, scarves, shirts, etc. The illustrations show treatments for a collar bone fracture and a broken rib. A fractured leg is immobilised by placing padding between the legs and using bandages to tie them together. Tie the feet together, too. Do not put a bandage directly over the fractured part. Treat a fractured hip bone similarly, with the knees and feet bound, and two thick bandages around the hips. If you suspect a fractured spine, you must make the patient lie absolutely still until an ambulance or doctor arrives. Cover him with coats. Any movement is dangerous.

Fractures can easily be made worse by rough or clumsy treatment. Try to keep the fracture quite still until medical help arrives.

Unconsciousness

If a patient is unconscious, check first that he is breathing. If not, give artificial respiration (see earlier). Always check his mouth, as it is easy for an unconscious person to choke. Clear his mouth (see method earlier) of vomit or loose teeth. Check for fractures. If you suspect a fracture, which makes it unwise to move him, concentrate on making sure he can breathe. Bend his head back so that the nostrils point upwards and keep his lower jaw open by pulling it down with the thumb. If there seem to be no complications, the patient should be gently placed into the recovery position illustrated. Send for help, and keep careful watch on the patient, particularly his breathing.

Summary

The following is a quick check list on how to behave when in a situation calling for first aid. If his position is safe, treat the patient where he is. Check his breathing. Check for choking. Check for bleeding. Reassure him. Dress any wounds. Immobilise any fractures. Treat for shock if necessary. Send for help.

44

The recovery position. The patient is on his side, head bent back, with face down. The upper arm and leg are bent; the lower arm and leg are stretched out.

Look after his property. If you have time, keep notes to help the doctor or police. Stay with him until medical help arrives.

Walking & Hiking

Walking for the sheer fun of it, for leisure and recreation, is one of the oldest outdoor pursuits in Britain. In the 18th century, walking was a national sport and the 'peds', the leading professional pedestrians who walked vast distances for wagers, were as well known as leading footballers are today. Many young people had to walk long distances because there was no alternative; Welsh students at Cambridge walked home to North Wales at the end of the summer term because they had little money and enjoyed walking for its own sake. In September, they walked back again to Cambridge for another year.

Students who walked for pleasure in the summer vacation might well cover as much as 950 kilometres, wearing most unsuitable dress by modern standards, such as satiny, tight-waisted breeches and soft leather shoes without a single nail in them. Coleridge, the poet, together with a friend, both of them 20 at the time, did one of these marathon walks from Cambridge in a wide circle through North and Central Wales.

A Scout hillcraft project under way on the High Peak Trail in Derbyshire, England. Scouts, working in pairs, check their maps at regular intervals and are alert to any change in weather patterns.

HIGH PEAK TRAIL

VISITORS ARE WELCOME TO USE THE TRAIL subject to the conditions and bylaws on the back of this notice.

THE LAND IS GRAZED NO DOGS EXCEPT ON A LEAD

Their route lay along muddy, unmade roads and pathways, across wet fields and over desolate mountains, following sheep trails, old cow paths and tracks. They had no maps and few signs to help them. It would seem a daunting task today in a summer of high temperatures and frequent storms with heavy rain.

There are several types of leisure walking. Rambling in the country at weekends tends to be an adult pleasure. Hiking, as such, is likely to be a Scout or Girl Guide activity with some special purpose, such as following Hadrian's Wall from Wallsend to Bowness, a distance of some 120 kilometres, and one of Britain's classic walks. A similar hike follows Offa's Dyke, from Prestatyn in North Wales to the Severn river, built by Offa, King of Mercia, in the latter half of the 8th century to keep the Celts in Wales. The Dyke is not that easy to find in places now, but it provides 270 kilometres of pleasant hiking using a combination of youth hostels and lightweight camp sites as stopping places. Scouts, Guides and youth hostellers have long enjoyed this route in either direction.

Youth hostelling is currently enjoying a boom and 277,000 members of the Youth Hostels Association (England and Wales) were out and about in 1976. The YHA caters especially for young people of limited means, although family membership is now growing fast and providing happy, healthy outdoor activity for young and old alike.

Lastly, there is more specialized walking such as fell-scrambling, which is almost a sport in tough terrain such as that found in Cumbria, Northumberland, North Yorkshire and other parts of Britain. This is hiking for very fit, experienced young men and women, but there is no reason why boys and girls should not try the easier slopes of, say, the Cumbrian fells.

Australian Scouts hiking in the outback wear broadbrimmed hats against sun.

Hiking equipment

The initial outlay on suitable equipment for hiking is considerably cheaper than for camping, unless it is intended to specialize in backpacking, that is, hiking or trekking on foot with ultra-lightweight gear. This can be very expensive, though need not be; everything is carried in the rucksack and camping is where the mood takes one in the hills and mountains. Youth hostelling costs very little and is probably the cheapest of all outdoor activities. Scout and Guide hiking tends to take the form of day hikes from home with a bus, coach or train journey included; there may also be day hikes from a tented base, such as 24-hour patrol adventure hikes with bivouac shelters overnight from the main summer camp.

The basic needs are simple: rucksack; sleeping bag (if necessary); sheet bag, or lining as it is more often called; personal kit; changes of clothing, including an extra pullover in case of colder weather; protective clothing for wet weather; maps; notebook and pencil for the daily log of time, distance, points of interest and expenses; camera; binoculars, if wished; compass; and a pedometer for recording exact mileage walked. Most hikers will carry two meals in one form or another, some emergency rations in

Basic gear for day hikes.

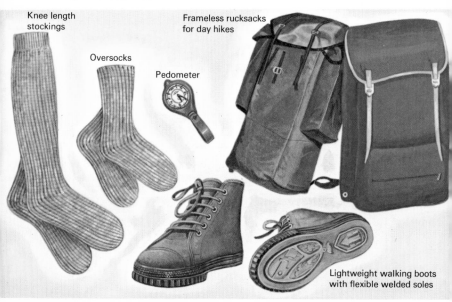

Knee length stockings

Oversocks

Pedometer

Frameless rucksacks for day hikes

Lightweight walking boots with flexible welded soles

Above: The Alps demand a high standard of outdoor skills; a circuit trek of Mont Blanc's glaciers.

Below: A weatherproof, outdoor jacket with four patch pockets, drawcord waist and built-in hood.

case they are enveloped by mist on a hillside or coastal estuary and have to 'bivvy' (make a temporary shelter, using a groundsheet if available), a lightweight water bottle and probably a lightweight, solid fuel boiling set for a hot drink or soup.

The hiker's personal gear starts with a string vest, cool in high summer and warm on colder days, since it traps a snug layer of warm air next to the skin but allows it to escape in summer. Comfortable, lightweight, warm trousers are preferable to shorts except in very high summer, since there is less exposure of vulnerable places, such as the back of the knees, to sunburn, less risk of exposure (and hypothermia) in winter and less risk of unpleasant insect stings (such as that from the *taons*, a large horsefly known throughout the Alps), scratches from brambles, and grazes and cuts from stone walls and paths. Long trousers also protect knees and thighs from brushburn on ropes, and all the ravages of 'burns' and tears on scree slopes in the hills.

There should be no restriction at the waist; wear a loose-fitting cotton, or cotton and wool mix shirt, and a warm pullover, such as a Shetland wool sleeveless slipover, with an anorak on top. Keep a warm, long-sleeved crew-neck type pullover in the same wool in your rucksack as a change. The anorak must be wind-proof above everything, with a built-in hood with drawcord. One of the most popular types is shown in the illustration on page 49; it has a zip-front opening with four large patch pockets with button-down

Britain's first youth hostels were set up in North Wales; Bryn Gwynant is very popular.

flaps, drawcord waist and elasticated wrists. Mittens are worn universally in colder weather. Walking boots should be strong and light-weight, with built-in tongues or one-piece uppers and made of supple leather or strong canvas with padded ankles and a non-slip sole and heel. Steel-crudded soles and heels are rarely seen among hikers now; they are strong and reliable but far too heavy and tend to draw heat from the feet in cold weather.

For longer hikes, when you will be carrying more equipment, you should have a rucksack with a light metal frame of some kind that fits the back like a glove when properly adjusted, yet carries a good load perfectly, with a current of air

Tanner's Hatch is typical of the rich variety of buildings converted to youth hostels.

circulating between the frame and your back. This prevents perspiration from 'seating', as it is called, in the small of the back, with the risk of chills as soon as walking is over for the day. Carrying straps, waist harnesses and shoulder pads all help to ensure pleasant walking; chrome, leather, foam rubber and nylon have all been combined cleverly to deal with the hiker's basic need for comfort.

Some anoraks are completely waterproof as well as windproof; my own anorak is of this type so that I need not carry a lightweight cape in addition. I prefer to have a lightweight PVC groundsheet in my rucksack to give me a dry place when I sit down for a meal or rest full-length, or to make a bivvy if it rains hard or I happen to be caught in some other temporary hazard.

The personal gear should include a good foot talc or a medicated all-purpose talc; the feet *must be washed and dried thoroughly* every evening on hike and talc should be applied to them both at night after washing and in the morning. Talc should also be sprinkled in the stockings. It helps to avoid blisters if a little white vaseline is rubbed on and in between the toes and also on the back of the heels. Oversocks to prevent scree or grit getting in between

The YHA arrange summer hostelling tours with experienced leaders on the Continent. Tours are graded to suit individuals. Brienz YH in the Bernese Oberland of Switzerland is one base.

Girls on a youth hostel trek in Argyll take a lunch break by a waterfall in Glencoe.

boot and stocking are folded over the top of the boot; there is no need to use talc in them. This daily foot drill is most important in all types of hiking, to ensure comfort. Keep toe nails trimmed square.

Youth hostelling

'Hike' is essentially a word of enthusiasm; a boy or girl can *walk*, *ramble* or *tramp* the outdoor trail but it is impossible to *hike* without a smile and a song, and keen, fresh, unpolluted air ruffling the hair! No single organisation knows this better than the Youth Hostels Association. Hostelling started as an idea in the mind of Richard Schirrmann, a German schoolmaster who

led school parties hiking and opened the first youth hostel, a castle in Westphalia, in 1909. Germany has some of the finest hostels in the world.

When you have had a wide range of experience of hostelling in various parts of your own country, it is time to think of adventures abroad. YHA adventure holidays are the answer for many. From a sound knowledge and experience of hillcraft, the young hosteller can go on to experience a special grade hostel, such as Pen-y-Pass, at the head of Llanberis Pass in Snowdonia; it is an ideal setting for the YHA climbing and mountaincraft courses included in its Adventure Holidays scheme.

Hiking on the Continent offers superb youth hostelling. Sometimes it may be combined with lightweight camping and the use of well-equipped mountain huts, for example in the Austrian Tyrol, the French, Swiss and Bavarian Alps, the Pyrenees, the Black Forest, Norway, the gentler slopes and wooded valleys in the Belgian Ardennes, and beautiful Normandy and Brittany in France.

Britain's first hostels were in North Wales; the impetus came from Liverpool, and the first of a chain of splendid hostels was set up by the Merseyside YHA in 1931. By 1955 the association had about 186,000 members and in 1977 this figure has grown to 277,000.

The hosteller has no idea what kind of a building awaits him or her

Canoeing is one of the many different hostelling activities which members can take part in. Skills are learnt in groups, each individual using a single-seater canoe.

when a 'yo ho' tour is planned; it could be a shepherd's bothy, a Norman castle, a watermill, glove factory, life-boat house, converted railway station or a former public house! The sheer variety is remarkable, but all youth hostels have much in common: they provide simple, inexpensive accommodation, food and fellowship for active young walkers and cyclists. There are separate dormitories and washing facilities for boys and girls, a common room and a kitchen where members may cook their own meals. At most hostels, meals cooked by the warden or his wife can be purchased.

Dormitories are furnished with adequate beds (usually two-tier), mattresses, pillows and blankets.

Each YHA member is advised to carry his or her own sheet sleeping bag, but these can be hired by the night at many hostels if preferred. Hostel rules are simple. On arrival, a member signs the house-book and hands over his or her membership card. A bed is allocated and bed-making is the first chore! After supper, most hostellers like to chat and exchange the day's experiences with other hostellers, who may well come from a dozen different countries. Hostelling is truly international. Common-room singsongs and impromptu entertainment are a feature of hostel life and often reach a high standard.

Next morning, about half an hour is spent helping with washing-up or cleaning duties, before the day's hike begins. A hosteller can stay three consecutive nights in one hostel, but many stay only one. Sometimes, working parties help to decorate hostels or take part in some local conservation scheme. 'Countryside Discovery' weeks have been a considerable success with YHA members in Britain. The pages of the British YHA quarterly journal *Hostelling News* are packed with information about hostelling projects and activities.

Scout and Guide hiking

The pattern of hiking in Scout and Girl Guide training follows its own individual method. Many Youth Hostel activities can and do follow the same approach; I have had considerable success with compass traversing and simple map-making in Dovedale, Derbyshire with parties of boys and girls based at a very fine hostel in Hartington Hall. The same projects worked just as well when carried out by Scouts camping in Dovedale and working from their tented base. If the project in hand is practical and really interesting then it may well be carried out from a combination of youth hostels and lightweight tents, on foot or by cycle. In Britain, many

Scout hikers know that hills, dales, fells and mountains must be treated with respect; hill walking is safe when map and compass have been thoroughly mastered.

Scouts and Guides are enthusiastic youth hostellers.

Scouts and Guides, and Scouts in particular, hike all the year round. Scout troops attached to a church often use a church hall for their weekly meetings, but they will do most of their training and activities outdoors. Open groups, which are not attached to any particular church, have their own head-quarters and troop rooms. In country areas these are often used, by advance arrangement, for over-night sleeping and resting by Scout hiking parties from city suburbs and towns in heavily populated areas. I have happy memories of exploring the Peak District of Derbyshire with Scouts; we stayed overnight, usually on bank holiday weekends, at several local Scout Group head-quarters in the area. We slept in sleeping bags, using hammocks which we had made ourselves and carried with us. All these expedi-tions were in months like November, March and early April, when camp-ing in Derbyshire is not advised.

My logbooks show Scout hikes in Lakeland, the Yorkshire Dales, the Pennine moorlands, the Dee and Conwy valleys in North Wales, and many valleys in mid-Wales, such as the Tanat, where the overnight stops were made at local Scout Group headquarters, often with splendid hospitality. Hammocks, wooden bunks in log cabins, and groundsheets and kampamats on the floor, were used.

Walking with a purpose

When you are out walking it is interesting to record how far you have gone. Mileage can be recorded accurately on a pedometer and it is always useful to know exactly how far you have walked and to plot the route on an Ordnance Survey 1 : 50 000 series map or maps. These maps give a magnificent picture of the British Isles with all the detailed information that walkers could pos-sibly require. A simple daily log-book is always needed. On winter nights these logs can be enlivened with colour photographs, souvenirs, receipts and picture postcards,

A Scout birdwatcher out hiking makes field observations for a World Conservation Badge project.

along with anything else that you have collected. Keep maps and log-books in a safe place, such as a bookcase with glass fronts, because their value will increase over the years and they may be used to provide inspiration for new generations of walkers and hikers.

In Australia a different pattern of hiking exists, in the form of chains of bushwalking clubs. Children are introduced to bushwalking by parents at an early age through family picnics, so that they grow up with feelings of complete security in the vast, open spaces of the bushland.

Australian boys and girls develop habits of sound conservation practice from their earliest years. Nature projects carried out in recent years include noting and drawing tree patterns, learning to distinguish trees by their bark, fruit and flowers, learning to arrange wild flowers in families and identifying plants by seedpods. Much field work has been done on finding the foods eaten by lizards and other bush creatures. Insect life histories have been worked out, and butterflies recorded and identified. Wild birds are identified on bush walks by footprints, call and flight; the feeding habits of wildlife have been recorded and, in the case of many birds, the methods of eating and dealing with natural food. Photography is encouraged.

These nature projects will be familiar to Scouts and Guides in many parts of the world. Finding out where birds roost in winter is one valuable project; starlings, for instance, will find a hole under the eaves of a large house and in no time will roost in the warm confines of a boarded roof, with nest sites to follow in the spring. Derelict cot-

A stream in limestone country may plunge over a precipice as at Hunt Pot in North Yorks, so take care!

Following the mountain railway track to the summit of Snowdon, in North Wales, makes an interesting walk.

tages in some parts of Britain, such as Wales, need to be approached with care since every one seems to have a large white barn owl in occupation somewhere, which may fly through a broken window in daylight, brushing the faces of startled young hikers.

Following a stream to its source or to its confluence with a bigger stream or river is never advisable. It can be incredibly dangerous in most parts of Britain. In North Yorkshire, way above beautiful Wharfedale, in pothole country, streams suddenly end at precipices or great, gaping, highly dangerous holes in the ground. In North Wales a great many hikers have followed the mountain railway track to the summit of Snowdon. If you go on such a hike you should take great care, for no mountain path is ever really safe; at least, it is best never to take chances because second chances may not occur at all.

It is just as easy to slip on a very dry, worn pathway in a hot, dry summer, as a muddy one in spring; and it is all too easy on a rough, heathery slope to go slipping and sliding over some rock face, causing yourself serious injury. This can happen in broad daylight in the finest of weather, so personal safety precautions need to be sound at all times. In Skye it is easy to cross a field path and suddenly be surrounded by Highland cattle! They can be distinctly unfriendly, and so can goats in West Wales, where as

Geology is a fascinating outdoor hobby which is easily combined with day hikes to quarries or beaches.

many as 20 to 25 are now kept at a time by small farmers.

If a spell of unsettled weather sets in, alternative programmes are needed. Rainy day activities need thinking about: a pack of cards, a tiny transistor for radio news and sports commentaries, a paperback book of puzzles of all kinds, all help. All hikers can take time off to enjoy pony-trekking, sailing, canoeing, outdoor skating, folk dancing, gliding, swimming and sheep dog trials. All these activities, and many more, are in the programme of Scouts, Guides and youth hostellers.

Do not neglect winter hiking. The traditional Boxing Day hikes, the walks in crisp, dry wintry air, with snow underfoot and ice on the loch, are as exhilarating as any summer trek and more enjoyable than the heat.

Some useful walking and hiking terms

arête narrow ridge of hard rock or snow at an angle

avalanche natural fall of ice or snow in quantity

beacon conspicuous hill of no great height

blanket thick mist or fog

chimney a vertical cleft in rock

chine a deep, wooded ravine leading to the sea

chockstone a large stone jammed in a chimney

clatter a noun of quantity: 'a clatter of hikers'

cleave a moorland coombe or valley

clinker a heavy nail in soft metal on the outside of older-style boots

commando a type of sole and heel which holds well on rock, snow and ice

cornice an overhang of snow on the crest of a ridge

couloir a wide furrow on a mountainside, in rock or snow

crampons a framework of sharp spikes for fastening to boot soles

crevasse a long cleft in a glacier

cut a canal

cwm (Wales), *corrie* (Scotland), *cirque* (Alps) a large, semi-circular hollow on the side of mountains

The wide valleys and fells of the Lake District offer ideal walking for larger parties.

Skiddaw (930 metres) gives impressive long-range views from the lesser fells around Keswick in the English Lake District; these fell walkers are returning to their youth hostel after a day hike.

caused by the scooping action of ice during the Ice Age

fell   wide stretch of hilly moorland

flash   a stretch of artificial water, such as a reservoir, clay pit etc.

glacier   natural river of ice moving very slowly down a mountain from high snow

glissade   a controlled slide down a snow slope

greenhorn   an inexperienced hiker

gully   deep open furrow on mountainside

knoll   a small hill

marathon   Scout hiking competition in teams of four

moraine   stone debris carried down a mountain by a glacier and left at the foot of the mountain

pack (American) or *pacquet* (French)   loaded rucksack

ridge-walking   hiking on a watershed at a uniform height on a ridge

scramble   hike in steep fell country

scree   great mounds of small stones, debris at the foot of crags and mountains

spur   projecting mountainside, clearly visible

stance   clear ledge or resting place on mountain.

traverse   hike across mountain face or down valley

verglas   thin coating of ice on rocks

watershed   line of demarcation between different valleys and river systems

Hillcraft

Hillcraft is an introduction to mountain camping and the great outdoor sports of rock climbing and mountaineering, which may well attract you in later years. They can be enjoyed in so many parts of the world that climbing is truly an international sport today; many climbers of all nationalities have conquered Mount Everest in the Himalayas since the first successful ascent by Edmund Hillary of New Zealand and Tenzing Norkey, a Sherpa, during Colonel John Hunt's 1953 Expedition.

Hillcraft can be practised as soon as you have mastered the skills of camping, hiking, youth hostelling, trekking and backpacking – that is, walking with a tent and lightweight equipment in a rucksack, finding overnight sites on the trail, and walking either for sheer pleasure or with some definite purpose or hobby in mind. Many young people live within easy reach of substantial hills, fells and the lower slopes of considerable mountains. Others have a rich heritage of moorland, wild rough country and lonely hill trails on their doorstep. All of these make worthwhile exploring. All demand great care and preparation.

The most important requirement

The high fells of Langdale, Yorkshire, provide superb fellwalking.

Camping in Glencoe, Argyll, in a chilly spring with rocks holding down tent pegs.

is to be fit and stay fit. This applies not only to the leader of any group of hikers, but to every member of the team. That word 'team' is vital. Hillcraft demands sound teamwork in the true traditions of Everest expeditions. No mountain is ever climbed without first-class teamwork. From the very beginning then, self counts last. Leaders of outdoor expeditions tend to come to the top naturally; their example and personal skill marks them out to their friends. If there are two or more potential leaders let them practise their skills in turn.

Keeping fit means eating good, well-prepared, simple food at regular times of the day, and getting plenty of sound exercise and sleep. Walking is the best exercise of all, so never take a bus or accept a lift in a car if you can walk in comfort to your destination and can get there in time. If you do not walk enough your legs lose their strength and resilience; you become flabby and short-winded, and your skin loses that magic glow which comes from lots of walking in the open air in all kinds of weather. The Americans discovered this when school children were found to be using cars too much; as soon as they started using their legs more, walking to and from school, and for pleasure at weekends, the muscles came back, and with them, abounding health.

Learning the principles

From the outset, the hill walker and camper must develop and maintain a deep interest in equipment. Great mountains today are climbed only with the best quality equipment. Mountain tents are made of special windproof fabrics as they have to stand up to the bitterly cold winds experienced, say, on Himalayan slopes at heights of 7,600 to 8,800 metres. Some have wide valances on the sides and ends so that heavy rocks can be placed on these to help keep the tents properly pitched. Sleeve openings fit inside each other so that several tents can be linked together in a kind of tunnel formation with the campers able to move from one tent to another through the 'tunnels'. In time you may have the experience of using such mountain tents.

Concentrate on essentials at this stage; gain as much practical experience as possible of hill walking and fell scrambling in the spring-to-autumn part of the year, according to local weather conditions. The first principle is that you never go out alone or in pairs in the hills, even in summer. The reasons are obvious. If a 'loner' gets injured, who is to know what has happened? If one of a pair meets with some accident, even a simple thing like a sprained ankle, which can happen so easily on a dusty, loose, hill trail, how can the one remaining person deal with the situation?

In general, four or six people is a good size for a small party in the hills. One person needs to be more experienced than the others and an obvious leader. I like a party of six for summer outdoor expeditions, with one of the party being a really experienced leader, probably a little older than the others, and with a sound second in command, also with experience. If the remaining four are fit, strong and good team members, able and willing to fit in with the lead given, and the majority wishes of the patrol on all projects in hand, then there is every reason to believe the hike will be very successful.

Pairs are always better than odd numbers on hill treks, and four or six are ideal for small expeditions. A good idea is to adopt the 'buddy' system, with every person responsible not only for his or her own personal performance but also having thought and care for one other person. If someone begins to flag, or gets the 'knock', a general feeling of exhaustion and weakness, then something can be done about it at once. It is easily cured with rest, glucose tablets and chocolate, or a hot drink or soup, with a substantial cheese sandwich and chocolate and dried fruit to follow. In the hills, twos are always company; odd numbers are not.

Fell walkers, wearing colourful clothing, climb above Red Tarn, Helvellyn in the Lake District.

Woollen balaclava helmet (can be worn as a peaked cap, as shown here)

Nylon rope

Helmet

A selection of the equipment required for the more advanced skills of rock climbing.

The Scout Association, with its vast experience of all outdoor activities, has wisely decided that the maximum size of a hill party should be *ten*, including *two* experienced leaders. This maximum size party is only advised, in fact, with low-level hikes, treks and journeys, that is, hikes which do not tackle anything much above 400 to 500 metres. 'Low level' in some cases in, say, Scotland, Wales and the Lake District is likely to be much lower than these heights, depending on the weather. If larger numbers are contemplated, then the group splits up into separate parties, usually in units of four, six or eight, each with experienced and trained leaders. This serves to emphasise that hills and the lower slopes of mountains must at all times be treated with respect. In Britain especially, and in the European Alps, weather patterns tend to change rapidly. In North Wales, for instance, which is a favourite outdoor choice for young people from all parts of Britain and

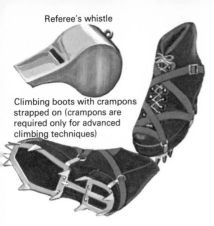

Referee's whistle

Climbing boots with crampons strapped on (crampons are required only for advanced climbing techniques)

the Continent (700 French boys and girls, and many large parties from Norway, Holland, Germany and Belgium in 1976 at one stage alone), the weather is variable at all times. A wet morning, with sea fret blowing in strength from the west, can be followed by a glorious afternoon with bright blue skies, scudding white clouds and a fresh breeze, and then by a misty evening with chilly ground conditions. All these patterns of weather we learn by experience.

In general, in Britain weather tends to be worse the higher you go, so there is no point in being over ambitious. A sound hill trail in high summer can be very difficult in the wet, muddy conditions of early autumn, or the very cold days of early spring with ice in every little hollow and rut underfoot. Imagine what it must be like up on top then! Imagine how much more experience and skill you will need before you can even think of walking and climbing up there, or carrying out even simple hill and fell walking in winter! All high-level work requires special equipment and clothing; rock climbing itself demands the use of ropes, karabiners, safety helmets, and much attention to equipment and food, apart from the personal skills of the leader, who carries a heavy responsibility at all times.

Boys, well trained in hillcraft, proceed to basic climbing techniques on Daw Crags, N. Lancs.

Personal equipment

You will see illustrated on pages 64 and 65 the sort of equipment that is needed for hill walking and fell scrambling in late spring to the end of summer in Britain. Always buy the very best gear you can afford. The right kind of equipment is far from cheap; it must stand the test of time and many treks across the hills and fells. This personal kit should be carried by each individual at all times.

Remember that colours are important in the hills. Do not wear outer gear that tones with your surroundings because it will not be visible from a distance and if you meet with a sudden emergency and need help, this could be vital. Browns and other drab colours are quite unsuitable. You need bright orange, bright yellow, striking blue and red clothing; this applies to all gear including sweaters, gloves, headgear, stockings, lightweight tents, if carried and used, and of course, rucksacks and anoraks or other outer jackets. Some vivid greens are now used very effectively for anoraks. I use a distinctive green outer jacket for bird-watching in the hills; it tones with the surroundings enough to make my movements inconspicuous, yet it could be seen easily if necessary on a trail.

Rucksacks are usually a bright red, green or blue nowadays. The red rucksacks I use for day hikes

Kent Scouts took a labrador dog to North Wales; it enjoyed hill walking too!

These Nottingham Venture Scouts enjoy a well-earned break with chocolate biscuits and a hot drink.

and longer trips can be seen from a long way off and they do add a real touch of gaiety and cheerfulness to the party or team on the hills.

Experienced climbers and mountaineers list six very important items in a personal hillcraft kit: the correct map, or maps, on the right scale for the area; a Silva compass; a whistle of the referee's type; an emergency food pack, which must contain a generous supply of glucose tablets; a small first-aid kit (see page 90); and a spare pullover. All are agreed that the most useful pullover is a long-sleeved, polo- or crew-neck type, in really warm yet lightweight wool. This list assumes that you already have the three essentials: boots, clothing that is both waterproof and windproof, and a rucksack.

Points to remember

In this chapter I have assumed that hillcraft will take the form of very active, small party, day hikes, or 2- or 3-day hikes with lightweight tents, or overnight youth hostel stops. You will probably be hiking in hilly but tough country, the lower slopes of Lakeland fells, or the moorlands and mountains of England, Wales, Scotland and Ireland, or their equivalents in Norway, the Continent, Australia and New Zealand. All this activity forms an *introduction* to outdoor projects in winter as well as spring, summer and autumn. Given time, you will improve in experience and fitness. There is all the time in the world for climbing when you are ready for it physically *and* mentally, and have

67

lots of outdoor experience in basic camping, hiking, hillcraft and youth hostelling.

Briefly, learn to watch the weather all the time. Morning fret and sea mist if you are on hills near the western coastline, rain in the hills (*intense* in the Lake District and persistent in Wales and Scotland), sleet, hailstones and wet snow in spring, even early summer, and the sudden onset of ground mist in mid-afternoon as the sun disappears are the things to watch for. Study the clouds and prevailing winds; learn to recognise wind and cloud patterns so that you can anticipate the weather for the next few hours ahead. Never go out on a hill project if the wind is variable, seeming to come from all quarters; it is often a sign of forthcoming gales. Listen to the latest weather forecasts, which you can dial on the telephone, because invariably they are more up-to-date than radio bulletins. The weather report is the same as that received by local RAF station pilots.

Plan the day's route carefully; never be afraid to abandon it and return to base by the shortest, safest route possible. These 'escape routes' are established practice in Scout hillcraft. Take your time in walking on gradients; go at the speed of the slowest member; although teams are always built up of pairs of about the same standard, there will usually be at least one member of a party still learning the game. Never split up and always re-form after any

obstacle on the route, such as a fall of scree and rock debris, has tended to scatter the team. It is important that *every* member knows that exhaustion must be avoided. You must also avoid hypothermia, for extreme cold and wet conditions, together with exposure to very cold wind, can lead quickly to death. This is dealt with in detail in the booklets recommended in the further reading list at the end of the book.

Remember that if any person in the party suddenly starts a cold, shivering fit, with stumbling, 'going

Advanced climbing techniques and experience of high-altitude camping are needed on mountain expeditions.

off the handle' at friends who try to help, an obvious loss of direction (due to disturbed vision) and other unusual symptoms, then immediate action must be taken. Stop at once and insulate the victim against any further heat loss: a lightweight tent can be erected if carried or a 'bivvy' made (a temporary bivouac or windproof shelter using any materials available) and the person popped into a polythene survival bag inside it. No massage, skin rubbing of any kind, or stimulants should be given. A quick, very hot drink, such as instant coffee with lots of condensed milk in it, or cocoa made with tinned milk and brown sugar, or a mug of soup, will probably revive mild cases. If, like me, you never take sugar and dislike sweet things, I recommend a meat extract in very hot milk. Doctors recommend rapid 'rewarming' in a hot bath, with rest to follow in a warm room; this may be possible back at the base, such as a youth hostel. Occurrences such as this are, fortunately, uncommon in well-prepared expeditions in the warmer months of the year, but sound hill-craft means that all are prepared.

Always leave full details of the day's plans with someone before setting out. These should include names, ages, and home addresses of all members, the route and project details, the time expected back and so on. Leave this with a responsible adult, youth hostel warden, Scout or Guide leader, police station, guesthouse, café, post office or local inn. Always report your safe arrival back at base to anyone left with details. Know where telephones are en route, including any mountain rescue posts or 'phones on wayside telephone poles, as in the Isle of Mull. They will probably never be needed, but how appalling if an emergency arose and you didn't know where they were!

Timing your trek

Naismith's Rule is a good guide to timing route progress. Allow four kilometres an hour in average hilly country plus one hour for every 450 metres of ascent, if the minimum of gear is carried. If carrying loads, allow $1\frac{1}{4}$ kilometres an hour plus an hour for 300 metres of ascent. The leader will ensure that the team knows the International Distress Signal (page 30) but this is only used by whistle, flare, torchlight or other means in real emergency.

Hikers near the end of a tough scramble to the top of Gordale Scar in Yorkshire.

Although cold conditions and mild exposure are the most common hazards of hill treks, especially in early spring or early autumn, it is essential to know that they can occur at any time in an average summer. Hailstones in May and July and

ing and using plenty of common sense.

Hill treks in high summer need to guard against the possibility of heat exhaustion. Carry only essentials in such weather. Do not overdo the length and scope of treks. Walk in the early part of the day and rest between 11.30 a.m. and 4 p.m. if need be, walking again in the cool of the evening. Wash and dry feet thoroughly every evening; use a foot talc, or a medicated foot powder on the feet and inside socks daily to avoid blisters.

If anyone shows signs of distress such as wilting in the heat, with great patches of perspiration on the back and sides of the body, stop at once. Headaches often accompany this condition and also eye disturbance. The skin is pale and the heavy loss of body fluids and salt causes a state of shock. Move the victim into shade and sponge the skin with cotton wool or whatever is handy. Get him to drink as much fluid as possible; fruit juices are ideal but often unavailable on hill trails. Every mug of fluid should contain the equivalent of half a teaspoon of salt. The victim will recover well.

Do not confuse heat exhaustion with heat stroke. Hikers wearing too many thick, *dark* clothes in humid conditions find their body heat cannot escape, and sweat is trapped between the layers of clothing. Dark clothing absorbs heat; light, airy, cellular clothing is far more healthy.

sleet blizzards in June or September, are not unknown on British hills and mountains. Driving winds with cold and thoroughly unpleasant heavy rain are possible at any time of year in the Lake District, parts of North Wales and many parts of Scotland. Avoid getting wet through by wearing really protective cloth-

Orienteering

Orienteering is a competitive sport which originated in Sweden at about the beginning of this century. It has now spread and is enjoyed by a growing number of people of all ages in Europe, Australia, Canada, U.S.A. and Japan. It is like a car rally on foot. The orienteers are given specially drawn detailed maps on to which a series of circles indicating the control points are marked. Using the map, and with the aid of a compass, the competitors have to find their way from point to point in the shortest possible length of time.

Above: A Silva compass
Below: Part of an orienteering map showing a short course.

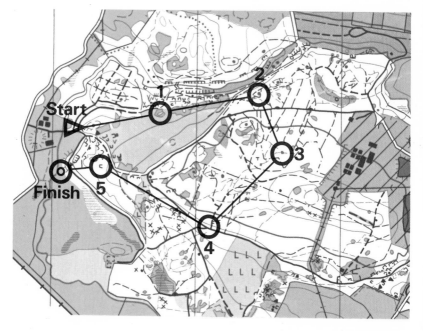

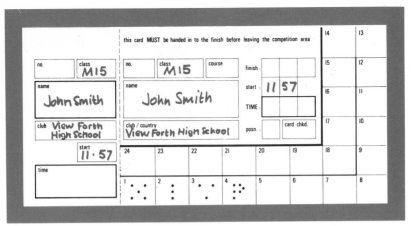

A typical control card showing the patterns made by the punches at the controls.

What happens at an event?

The competitions take place mainly in forests, parks or woods. When you arrive at the event you will report to *registration* for your course. There are classes for all ages from boys and girls under ten to men and women over fifty! At registration you will collect your map, control card and control descriptions sheet. You will also be given a start time, as competitors start at minute intervals in order to prevent following. You will then make your way to the start where you will be called up a few minutes before your start time.

When the starter blows his whistle you run to the master maps and carefully copy your course on to your map. Remember that a mistake in copying down the controls will make it very difficult for you to

```
M15 course  4.5km  Code

1 Pond                  26
2 Path Junction         45
3 Knoll                 32
4 Crag foot (W end)     62
5 Stream bend           51
6 Ruin, N corner        73
7 Gate                  99

Follow streamers 200
metres to finish
```

A control description sheet

complete the course, so take care. Now it is off to find the first control. When you find it, you will see a control marker hanging by the feature. Check the code letters on the marker with the ones on your description sheet and if they are correct, punch your control card with the special needle punch to show that you have been at the control. If you read the map carefully you will soon be at the last control and the way from here to the finish is usually marked by streamers.

As you cross the line your time will be noted and your control card collected. The officials will check your card to see that you have been at the correct controls and then work out the time you have taken. Your result will then be displayed with those of other members of your age group.

What equipment do I need to start?

Beginners usually wear old jeans, sweaters and anoraks with boots or training shoes on their feet. The only rule is that your arms and legs must be fully covered to prevent you catching any infection from scratches. In addition, you must carry a whistle for use *only* in emer-

Control marker and punch

gencies. The other things you will need are a polythene bag to hold your map and a pen to copy down the controls from the master maps. A compass of the Silva or Suunto type will be useful but is not essential.

What are the maps like?

The maps are specially drawn at large scales so that as much detail as possible can be shown to enable the orienteer to navigate skilfully round the course. Some of the main symbols used on orienteering maps are shown on page 76. Notice especially

Spectators enjoy the sunshine as they watch the finish of an orienteering event.

that open ground is shown as yellow and also notice the symbol for 'out of bounds' areas.

Simple techniques

Map reading

Elsewhere in this book the basic ideas of map reading are described. When you are orienteering, the main rule is to try to know where you are on the map the whole time you are competing. At first, the easiest way to do this is to try to find the controls by following 'handrail features' such as paths, streams, fences and the edges of fields wherever possible. Try also to find an 'attack point' close to the control, such as a road junction, which can be easily found. By doing this you will keep the distance when you will have no handrail features as short as possible.

Route choice

There is no set way for you to go between controls and you will have to decide from the map which way looks quicker. In the lower map on page 77, for example, do you go over the hill, or take the longer route round the path? It is good practice to try to spot as many routes as you can between controls when you go home after the event.

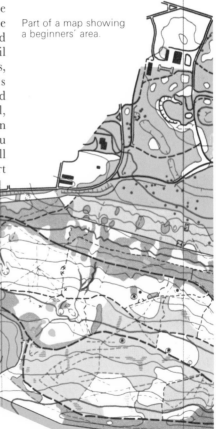

Part of a map showing a beginners' area.

Contour	Crossable wide stream	Open land	Wall	Dirt road
Steep bank	Crossable stream	Semi-open land	Cart track	Crossable fence
Small gully	Less distinct ditch	Vegetation: Slow running	Footpath	Uncrossable boundary
Depression	Uncrossable marsh	Vegetation: Difficult to run	Small path	Crossing point
Pit	Open marsh	Vegetation: Fight	Narrow ride	Building
Dangerous crags	Wooded marsh	Forest runnable in one direction	Narrow ride open	Settlement
Crags	Water tank	Felled area	Narrow ride heavy going	Ruin
Boulder	Well	Orchard	Wide ride	Small tower
Lake	Spring	Very distinct forest edge	Railway	Fodder rack
Uncrossable river or stream	Footbridge	Road	Power line, Skilift	Special small man-made features

A selection of the map symbols used internationally for orienteering maps.

Compass

The compass is a useful aid to the orienteer but it will not find the controls on its own. On page 19 there is information on how to use the compass. Remember that on the special orienteering maps the grid lines are set to magnetic north and

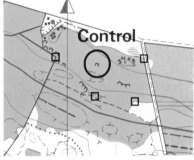

Attack points, such as those in squares on the map above, are points which can be easily found near controls and are used as starting places for the final section of a leg to a control.

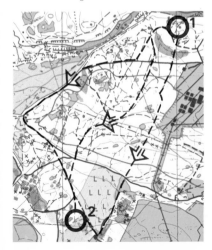

Route choice – which would be faster?

this means that no adjustments are necessary when going from the map to a bearing or vice versa.

How far?

The normal scales used on orienteering maps are 1:10 000, 1:15 000 and 1:20 000. It will be easier to think of distances if you can remember the following:

1:10 000, 1 centimetre on the map is equal to 100 metres on the ground.
1:15 000, 1 centimetre on the map is equal to 150 metres on the ground.
1:20 000, 1 centimetre on the map is equal to 200 metres on the ground.

Types of competition

Cross-country orienteering

This is the main type of event. Competitors start at one minute intervals and then have to visit a series of control points in a set order. At the end, the person visiting the controls in the fastest time is the winner.

Score orienteering

The check points on a score event are given points according to how far they are from the start. Competitors are then allowed a set time in which to gain as many points as possible. Penalty points are taken off for every extra minute used by the orienteer if he or she is out for more than the time allowed.

Relay events

Teams made up of three runners compete over shorter, cross-country orienteering courses and hand on to their team mates just as they do in an athletics relay.

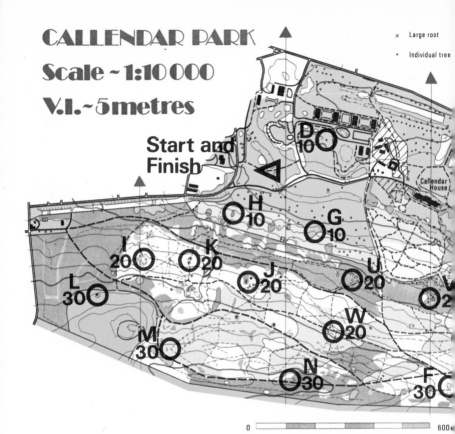

CALLENDAR PARK
Scale ~ 1:10 000
V.I. ~ 5 metres

× Large root

• Individual tree

Start and Finish

Callendar House

D 10
H 10
G 10
I 20
K 20
J 20
U 20
V 2
L 30
W 20
M 30
N 30
F 30

0 ⸻ 600m

Night orienteering

To make it more difficult some special events are held at night. Competitors usually use headlamps like those worn by miners.

Duke of Edinburgh's Award Scheme

Orienteering can be counted as part of the Duke of Edinburgh's Award Scheme, either on the Fitness section or in the Interest section.

Headlamps are worn for night events.

Open	Walk or Fight
Semi-Open	Vegetation boundary

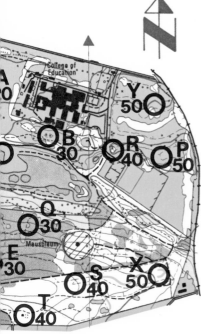

Permanent orienteering courses

In many countries there is an easy way to try orienteering by following the permanent courses set up in parks and woods. Map packs containing all the necessary information can be bought at places such as forest centres and sports shops. You can take as long as you like to find the control points, which are usually wooden posts with an orienteering marker painted on the top. On finishing the course there is, in most cases, an address to send the control card to if you want a certificate. Wayfaring schemes like this are run in Britain by the Forestry Commission and the British Orienteering Federation, and widely as TRIM O-L in Scandinavia.

A junior orienteer at a control point.

Age classes for competition

Men		Women
M10	10 years and under	W10
M12	11–12 years	W12
M13	13–14 years	W13
M15	15–16 years	W15
M17	17–18 years	W17
M19	19–21 years	—
—	19–34 years	W19
M21	21–34 years	—
M35	35–42 years	W35
M43	43–49 years	W43
M50	50 years and over	W50

Course lengths

As the terrain over which orienteering competitions are run is very varied, the competition courses are planned to take a certain time to run rather than be of a certain length. The examples below give some idea of course lengths for different age classes.

$\left.\begin{array}{l} W_{12} \\ M_{12} \end{array}\right\}$ 30 minutes 2–3 kilometres

M15 50 minutes 3–5 kilometres
W17 60 minutes 3–5.5 kilometres
M17 60 minutes 4–7 kilometres

Training exercises

To do well, an orienteer must be fit, but he must also practise to improve his navigation. Two examples of exercises used for training are given below.

Map memory

Here the orienteer has to memorise the route from A to B by looking at a small piece of map displayed at the control point. No map is carried on the course. This exercise is designed to give the orienteer confidence so that he or she does not find it necessary to stop too often to read the map during competitions.

Line event

The orienteer has to follow *exactly* the line which he copies on to his map from a master map, and then mark on the positions of controls

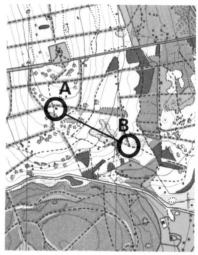

A piece of a map used for map memory.

when they are found. It is extremely important to navigate very carefully when doing this type of exercise because the controls that the orienteer must find are usually very small compared with those used in competition. This exercise is useful for making the orienteer follow the map with care.

Line training exercise showing hidden controls.

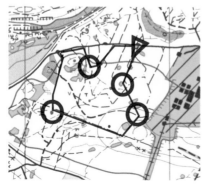

Golden rules

1 *Always report to the finish even if you do not complete the course.* If you do not do this the organiser may spend hours in the forest searching for you while you are safely at home.
2 Follow the Country Code and respect other people's property.
3 Keep quiet in the forest. Only blow your whistle if you are injured or lost and no one else is around.
4 Do not follow the person in front, he may be lost too!

An experienced junior orienteer

Useful addresses

To find out more about orienteering in the area in which you live write to the appropriate address below.

British Orienteering Federation,
Lea Green, Matlock, Derbyshire, England.
Irish Orienteering Association,
c/o 11 Lower Montenutte, Cork, Ireland.
Orienteering Federation of Australia,
P.O. Box 257, Camberwell, Victoria, Australia.
New Zealand Orienteering Federation,
New Zealand Herald, P.O. Box 32, Auckland, New Zealand.
Danish Orienteering Federation,
Brøndby Stadion, 20 Idraettens Hus, 2600 Glostrup, Denmark.
Norwegian Orienteering Federation,
Hauger Skolevie 1, 1346 Gjettum, Norway.
Swedish Orienteering Federation,
Box 43020, 10072 Stockholm, Sweden.
Swiss Orienteering Commission,
Landstr. 56, 8803 Ruschlikon, Switzerland.
French Orienteering Federation,
91 Rue du Faubourg, St. Denis, 75010 Paris, France.
Belgian Orienteering Federation,
c/o M. duRoisin, 40 Rue de la Brasserie, 4280 Hannut, Belgium.

Camping

Camping is a great outdoor adventure. It provides a simple, inexpensive means of getting to know the finest scenic parts of Britain, Europe and the Mediterranean, North America, Australasia and many other countries and continents at first hand. The personal horizons of boys and girls are widened as they gain more and more experience in being self-reliant in the open air. There is, however, far more to camping than just learning to live with other people under canvas. You will learn to share any hazards of weather that might occur, and the fun of cooking food in the open air and improving personal skills in so many different ways.

In countries with a cool temperate climate, such as Britain, camping is possible all the year round, but in practice the camping season tends to start at Easter and end in late September. Winter camping is for specialists, as it demands considerable experience and equipment which is expensive and more suited to use by adults. Boys and girls can hike all the year round,

Argyll is a fine choice for lightweight camping in Scotland at any time in spring, summer or early autumn; this site on Loch Etive is well sheltered from the prevailing winds.

A secluded camp site in the beautiful Tanat valley at Llanrhaeadr-ym-Mochnant, Denbighshire; the site provides a base for exploring the Berwyn range on day treks.

but early experience of camping and learning its technique is best acquired in spring, summer and the beginning of autumn. There is plenty of time for more advanced forms of camping later on when you have become thoroughly proficient.

First of all, the novice camper must learn to fit into the exhilarating landscape all around him or her; Man is only part of this extensive vista and from the very beginning, the camper must learn the skills of conserving the natural resources of the world in which he or she lives. All other living creatures have as

much right to exist in this environment. The sheer realisation of this simple fact is one of the great joys of camping and it comes in the first season of outdoor experience. Coming to terms with oneself, knowing limitations and the extent of personal skills, and then improving them, is good for all of us. It is easier to do this in camp than almost anywhere else.

Camping is not a way of life, but a means of getting more out of life and in this chapter we hope to show readers how to set about it from the beginning and gain lasting pleasure.

Choosing a tent

There are many ways to enjoy camping. Holiday camping by the sea appeals to many, especially on the Continent. Sites are controlled by local authorities; water, electricity, meal facilities and impromptu entertainments are features of such camp sites. Personal camping, on the other hand, provides more lasting enjoyment for boys and girls using lightweight, personal kits and travelling on foot, by cycle or by using the many forms of public transport, such as train, coach, bus, steamship and plane. One popular method involves parents with family cars who take campers to some selected area and arrange to meet them at a rendezvous on a later date.

Lightweight gear is the prime choice of all personal campers. It takes time and money to build up a personal kit that is going to last for years. Weigh up the facts carefully. An all-purpose kit can be built-up that is suitable for field camping inland, holiday camping on a farm by the sea in a breezy situation, fell scrambling in spring in rough, hilly terrain, camping on rock-hard ground in summer, or camping in dismally wet and chilly weather. Modern campers can choose a tent that will survive all these conditions, that is light in weight yet thoroughly

Explorer tents are ideal for novices. Simple in design and easy to erect, with sewn-in groundsheets, the Junior (right) sleeps two and the Senior (shown below with flysheet) three.

reliable, and will take two people comfortably or three if necessary.

A flysheet is a worthwhile extra. It makes the tent cooler in summer, and warmer in colder weather. It doubles the life of the tent, but does add considerably to the weight carried. Sooner or later a flysheet is a good investment but it is not necessary while basic skills are being mastered. Before buying a tent study the catalogues of manufacturers of international repute. Always buy the very best tent you can afford. Indeed this applies to all equipment but especially to tents because they are the basic temporary home. Illustrated on these pages are some tents of proved design; they are easily erected and dismantled. You will soon learn to talk about 'pitching camp' as tents are put up, and 'striking camp' when they are taken down! Pitch a new tent on the lawn

The Good Companions Standard model with flysheet is a world-famous tent. Ideal for two people with upright pole, or three if angle poles are used as here.

at home; do it many times until you can handle the tent as easily as you can a bike. Put the garden hose on it and see what it is like when wet.

Sewn-in groundsheets, angle poles and elastic-end guylines will all be useful in time. Camping is still fun with simple personal ground-

The larger, sturdy, ridge style of tent, such as the one pictured here, is the type most often used by Scout and Guide patrols at weekend and summer camps. Tent poles may be wooden or the lighter alloy type.

sheets and the minimum of gear. Scouts learn patrol camping from their earliest days in a troop, with patrol tents of varying types, but personal 2- and 3-man lightweight tents are also seen at every Scout troop's summer camps.

Personal equipment

Start with a basic tent that can be used by brothers, sisters, cousins and friends, for camping often becomes a family pastime. Many families acquire two or three tents and like nothing better than camping on the lawn at home in hot weather. This way skills are learned quickly and easily.

Personal groundsheets need to be lightweight, and very waterproof. PVC, oiled cotton or nylon are used in modern groundsheets; taped edges and strong eyelets make for

all-purpose toughness. They all fold up compactly and neatly: 183 × 76 cm is the standard junior size. The same groundsheet is light enough to carry on hikes; it may well make a fine temporary bivouac tent in mist or storms if used against a wall.

The next essential is a sleeping bag. Here again, cost is the factor that determines the final choice. Convertible bags are zipped down one side and across the end and can thus be used as quilts on beds at home in the winter, which helps the family budget. A bag in the medium price range of most catalogues will be lightweight, warm and have a sound, cambric or nylon cover; it is essential to use a sheet lining bag because it greatly lengthens the life of the bag and cuts down on expensive dry cleaning bills. Sheet linings make for hygiene, an important point in camping technique, and are

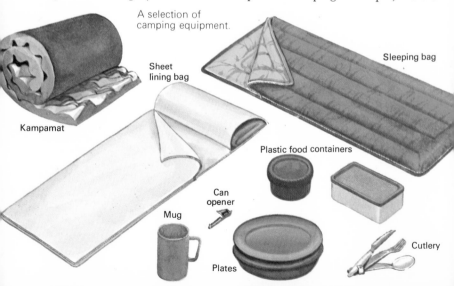

A selection of camping equipment.

Sheet lining bag

Sleeping bag

Kampamat

Plastic food containers

Can opener

Mug

Cutlery

Plates

easily laundered at home. A pillow is not essential but a simple air type is a luxury many campers enjoy; spare clothing in the pillow container attached to the head of the bag makes a good pillow.

Longer summer camps, such as an annual holiday camp of two or more weeks on a farm by the sea, are more comfortable if a kampamat is used; this is a white foam plastic mat used to provide insulation and comfort between the sleeping bag and groundsheet. Kampamats roll up neatly and should be kept at the very top of the packed rucksack with the groundsheet, which is always the first item to be unloaded.

Cooking equipment is best shared between two or three campers. Sometimes a wood fire may be used but a conventional primus stove, burning paraffin, or a Camping Gaz stove, with throwaway cartridge

Kubex oven
(folds flat)

Pyramid
toaster

Paraffin
stove

Solid fuel boiling set

Gas cartridge stove

Grip handle for use
with canteen set

Kettle

Cooking canteen

Water bottle

Assorted collapsible
water carriers

Canvas collapsible
water carrier

fuel containers, is essential. Two campers can get by on a 0·3 litre (fuel capacity) primus but three will need the 0·6 litre size. Learn how to operate and use it at home. Always ensure spares for stoves are carried (prickers, spanner, box, solid meths for priming, matches in waterproof box, Gaz cartridges).

There are a large variety of pots and pans to choose from; a selection of those available is shown on page 87. Water carriers are plastic, lightweight, even collapsible and foldaway in design. Food containers are also plastic and lightweight. 'Eating irons' are a camper's personal choice; experienced campers usually take a dual-purpose knife with serrated blade, a fork, dessert spoon, teaspoon, eggspoon and cup, and a kitchen tablespoon for cooking purposes. A reliable can-opener is essential. A medium-sized enamel or hard plastic mug for drinking and a small-sized one for cooking (one

A rucksack for lightweight camping with aluminium frame, side pockets and a map pocket on the flap.

mug between two) should complete the basic cooking kit required by campers.

A personal first-aid kit is essential at all times; never be without one. Keep it handy in the toilet bag in a suitable plastic box or tin with stout

Rucksack packing chart

Place all your gear and food to be carried on a table and sort it into six heaps as shown in the chart opposite. Leave the items which are to be packed outside the rucksack alone for the time being. If your rucksack has its main compartment or pocket divided into two – which is very useful in wet weather, when you may well be packing dry and wet, or damp things, as you can place them in different pockets – make certain the weights in the two halves are roughly equal. Otherwise you will have balancing problems! If your rucksack is of the more conventional pattern with one main sack, follow the chart and pack the bottom half with the gear you are unlikely to want as soon as you pitch camp.

Rucksack packing chart

Temporarily outside rucksack on top when not being worn

Sweater, pullover or anorak (waterproof outer jacket)

Always carried outside, below rucksack

Tent with compact pole arrangement, protected by waterproof tentbag; if 2 or 3-man tent, spread load to ensure equal weights

Main sack: one half if divided, or bottom half of single sack

Sleeping bag
Plimsolls, sandals or similar footgear
Plastic bags containing spare clothing, underwear, pyjamas etc., handkerchiefs
Sleeping bag and cotton sheet lining can be packed whenever in transit in a waterproof lightweight cotton bag with draw-cord neck

Main sack: one half if divided, or top half of single sack

Toilet bag
Mug and deep plate (if too big to fit in outside pocket)
Cooking stove, wrapped in cloth in its tin box, duster or cloth bag; cooking canteen also wrapped up or in bag with draw-cord neck
Camera in case/films
Groundsheet at top, covering all items snugly

To carry in pockets of anorak, if worn, and/or outside pockets of rucksack

All-purpose pocket knife (inside handkerchief if in rucksack)
Matches in waterproof tin with elastic bands round it, or book matches in waterproof tin or plastic bag
Personal toilet paper in plastic bag
Money, diary or identification card, travel tickets
Spare money for phone calls in plastic bag
Personal first-aid kit, which must be small; include water purifying tablets
Map and compass
Length of nylon cord for clothes line, in tent or outside

Remaining outside pockets of rucksack

Repair kit for clothes and tent, basics only
Shoe-cleaning kit, bootlaces
Small pieces of firelighter for wood fires, in fireproof tin
Emergency foods (glucose tablets, chocolate, dried apricots, artificial sweeteners if used, salt . . . to make small, compact pack)
'Eating irons' and midget can-opener (unless on pocket knife)
Plates (only if large pocket roomy enough, otherwise top of rucksack kit under flap)
Torch or flashlight (keep spare bulb and batteries in first-aid kit)
Spare socks or stockings
Fuel for stove (long outside pocket if fuel in polythene bottle)

Personal lightweight kit

A typical lightweight kit for hike-camping, trekking, bushwalking, backpacking, call it what you will so long as it is camping on the move, with a lightweight kit.

This list assumes that two people will be camping together and therefore sharing the weight of the tent, groundsheet and cooking canteen.

Figures below are average weights in kilograms

Lightweight, two-man, wedge-style tent, suitable for all purposes, all weathers (each)	1·2
Rucksack: nylon sac on aluminium frame	1·4
Lightweight oiled cotton on nylon groundsheet (each)	0·45
Lightweight sleeping bag. Sheet lining optional but recommended	2·0
Simple cooking canteen (each)	0·50
Large plate, mug, knife, fork, teaspoon and can opener (unless on knife carried with personal gear)	0·2
Meta boiling set, fuel, matches	0·35
Long sleeve pullover; spare clothing, including socks, shorts and T-shirt	0·8
Ultra-lightweight footwear change, e.g. plimsolls, moccasins	0·4
Two lightweight handtowels	0·45
Toilet bag, soap and first-aid kit	0·45
Emergency/survival kit, with glucose tablets, suitable food, repair kit for tent and clothes, and a length of nylon cord	0·45
Correct map(s) and compass	0·08
Torch, spare battery and bulb (Scout torch with right angle lens suggested; see page 31)	0·2
Waterproof anorak	1·13
Personal gear in wallet (diary, note-book, pencil, small camera etc.)	0·25
Aim at total including food	**10 kg**

If using lightweight cape or mac instead of anorak the weight will be approx. 0·45kg

elastic bands round it. The kit should contain the following items: washable plasters in assorted sizes for blisters, cuts and grazes; lint or gauze for dressings; acriflavine cream for burns and cuts; midge repellents; water-purifying tablets; aspirin for pain and headaches; a wide crêpe bandage; safety pins; cotton bandages; eyebath (plastic); and a small pair of scissors.

The rucksack is a vital part of every camper's kit. In time, a camper will probably have two rucksacks: a small, compact, lightweight nylon rucksack for day hikes and expeditions and a larger, stronger rucksack with a metal frame, for weekend camping and projects involving far more time with a tented base. The small rucksack should be able to hold a lightweight groundsheet and a waterproof or anorak, if the day demands it, with enough food for two meals, plus emergency rations and facilities for making a hot drink or soup, such as a meta boiling set (a small pan with self-contained burner using solid meths fuel tablets) or a simple 'tommy' cooker. A small first-aid kit, binoculars (if wished), camera, notebook and pencil, and a map in the zipped outside pocket completes the day pack. I use such a rucksack all the time on bird and animal watching treks; it is bright red with wide, comfortable carrying straps to fit the shoulders. If necessary, in case of emergency, the bright red colour could be seen clearly against the

Date checked and aired	Tent	Rucksack	Sleeping bag	Other gear
October **24th**	✓	✓	✓	✓
November **22nd**	✓	✓	✓	✓
December				
January				
February				
March				
April				

natural colours of vegetation and bare rock or soil, or the stark whiteness of snow.

Rucksacks are an investment; once again, buy the best at the beginning, because with care it is going to last for years. Every help is given to personal shoppers at camp suppliers to ensure that they buy the right size rucksack for their physical build; if buying by mail order then do make certain that advice has been taken from experienced campers or youth leaders first.

A suitable all-purpose rucksack for campers is a large capacity, divided sack in nylon, such as that shown in the illustration on page 88. A divided sack is most useful in wet weather for keeping wet and dry things apart and it also enables soiled and clean clothing to be separated. This rucksack has four side pockets, a map pocket on the flap and a reliable lightweight aluminium frame. The use of tubular frames with a platform base enables the sack to be carried high on the shoulders, the best way of all, and also keeps the load upright when the rucksack is taken off. Girls find shoulder pads and sponge-filled nylon shoulder harnesses very comfortable to wear.

Looking after your kit

When the personal kit is complete, ensure that identification marks are placed on every item; tents, clothing, sleeping bag and so on can have name tapes sewn-on, like school clothing, with a telephone number, but these should always be placed in inconspicuous places where rain, wear and tear will not damage them. The majority of camping items can be identified by personal emblems of one kind or another: for many years, I placed my three initials in morse on all my gear. I used nonpoisonous, hard enamel green paint on many items including the base of cups and plates, and an indelible paint on my rucksack and groundsheet. My tent could be identified in several ways in case a sewn-on name tag was removed. Unfortunately, there is a thriving market in secondhand camp gear, so every care must be taken to prevent loss, damage or theft. Once the kit is well-marked, the next step is to insure it for its full value with a reliable company, and to maintain the policy with any additions as necessary.

The kit will give years of pleasure if it is well cared for; never run the risk of mildew ruining anything. This unpleasant mould flourishes in damp, airless conditions. Tents are often taken down wet or damp when camp is struck, and packed temporarily for the journey home in polythene bags in the rucksack. Once home, they must be dried immediately, not in a warm room at all, but a cool, dry room with plenty of air circulating. A good idea is to place brown paper over the banisters and hang the tent loosely over them until dry; a tent is dry when the *seams* are dry, not the fabric. Learn to test dryness by feel, so that it becomes the accepted way to keep valuable camping gear.

Brush all mudspots and splashes off valances and tent doorways; this is best done with a light clothes brush when the tent is thoroughly dry. Ensure there is no dust or grit in rucksack seams and pockets; hang the sack upside down until it is quite dry all over. Clean tent pegs, cooking gear and especially the stove. During winter, or other times when the kit is not in use, the entire kit should be inspected every month. Air the tent, using the banisters again if possible, and the groundsheet and rucksack. Use the stove and canteen in the kitchen occasionally to practise cooking skills. Shake and air the sleeping bag un-

A weekend Scout patrol camp site with plenty of natural shelter, wood and water.

less it is a convertible quilt and in use in the home. Carry out any temporary repairs and adjustments that may be necessary on any item.

Scout and Guide camping

The Scout and Guide movements have been enormously successful since they were founded by the first Lord Baden-Powell (1857–1941) in 1908 and 1911 respectively. The emphasis on character training through healthy outdoor activities leads naturally to good citizenship and loyalty, integrity and reliability. The keynote in all Scout training is camping and hiking (in various guises). No one person has ever done more to influence young people through voluntary, adventurous outdoor activities than 'B-P'.

Scout camping skills, common to more than a hundred Scouting countries in the free world, were proved at the 14th World Jamboree held in Norway in the summer of 1975. On that occasion, some 1,500 patrols of eight boys each, selected by computer to ensure a thorough mix from the 18,000 boys representing 104 countries in camp, carried out 'The Great Adventure Hike' in mountains at a height of over 1,000 metres. The boys camped together as patrols, living off Nature's larder, and carrying out dozens of varied projects. As an experiment into the standards of Scout camping skills in the 70's it was a remarkable success.

The basis of Scout camping, and

Camping is part of Girl Guide training; annual summer camp is the highlight!

also its sister movement, the Girl Guides (in some parts of the world they are already one movement), is the patrol unit, with a well-trained patrol leader taking full charge of five to seven boys and giving them a camp programme of adventure and achievement. Team work is the basis of training. The ideal unit is the mobile patrol, carrying out projects and activities of all kinds from a tented base. Camp life is busy, lively, friendly and strenuous. The essence of Scout training is that the skills of camping are mastered so that hobbies, service to others, and conservation of natural resources can be practised.

A Scout troop consists of a number of patrols, usually four, who come together for an annual summer camp in July/August as part of the troop programme. The patrols have many patrol camps throughout the season. The Guides have a very similar system. Cub Scouts (the junior branch of Scouting) are aged 8 to 11 and camping is also part of their training. Scouts are aged 11 to 15; at 16 they become Venture Scouts, and may learn advanced camping techniques, climbing, mountaincraft and water adventure on rivers, lakes, canals and the open sea, all with camping as the basic skill in the project under way.

Venture Scouts travel the world meeting and camping with other Scouts, learning to live with boys of different nationalities to their own as a basis of world understanding. The Girl Guides, through the Brownies, Guides and Rangers, go along with them all the way, and many joint ventures take place. Scout and Guide camping has reached a very high standard, but it has never lost its magic appeal to individual boys and girls.

Lightweight camping

Lightweight camping is by far the most enjoyable way to get the most out of camping. Good camping is mobile camping and this can only be achieved with lightweight kit. Then, with experience and the mastery of technique and skills, which are not difficult to acquire and develop, camping takes on a new dimension of special appeal to young people today.

Boys and girls from all over the world will find many opportunities to camp and walk in the beautiful British countryside, the Australian bush and the magnificent scenery of

Weight must be kept to a minimum in cycle-camping. Gear is carried in panniers which should be evenly balanced over a rear wheel carrier. Sleeping bag roll and tent can be strapped across panniers and tent poles may be strapped to crossbar. You may also use front panniers for articles such as food and cycle repair kit.

New Zealand. The National Parks of the United States, the grandeur of British Columbia and other parts of Canada, Scandinavia, the Arctic, and the vast expanses of Africa, Eurasia, and South America will all be brought within easy reach of each other by supersonic flight. Lightweight kit will move with the needs of the times naturally.

Mobile camping means camping on foot with lightweight kit carried high on the back, which is why the Americans call it backpacking; they use the word 'pack' instead of 'rucksack', which itself is a German word, from *rücken*, meaning back, and *sack*, meaning bag. A camper who follows a trail or route, camping lightweight as he or she goes, is a backpacker.

In the same way, mobile camping includes camping in the mountains, camping by water using canoes and small boats, camping by cycle, and four-wheel camping with a small, reliable car or van. The scope is vast and many winter nights can be spent reading about the problems and techniques needed in these areas of activity. Sooner or later, you will probably find yourself combining special interests and hobbies with camping and hiking. Watching and recording wildlife, both birds and animals, making maps, studying landscape in all its forms and Man's adaptation to it, and the conservation of all natural resources, have always been life interests for me. I have been able to follow them

Camping by water using canoes is a form of lightweight camping. Kit is stowed at either end of the canoe.

without difficulty, thanks to hiking and mobile camping.

Lightweight tents need special care in pitching; never allow creases or folds to spoil the pitch of a tent, instead, look for a better site. Bad pitching puts undue stress on the guys and seams, and causes tears in the fabric. Pitch a tent so that the pegs or long steel *pitons*, used when camping on the Continent for greater stability in sandy ground, are in alignment with the seams, again to avoid strain. Flat boulders help a tent to take wind stress, so long as they are placed on metal pegs to avoid chafing nylon guylines. Never pitch below trees, which may result in stains from leaf drip in rain, or roosting birds. To avoid damage, never wear shoes inside a tent. Avoid touching the fabric when camping in wet weather without a flysheet. Cook near the tent if necessary, in a sheltered position, using a metal windshield or rocks to shield a pressure stove; ensure complete safety from fire at all times and do not allow stove heat to damage the tent's waterproofing.

Tidiness is the secret to lightweight camping; it becomes second nature. Follow the same routine for packing as that already outlined, with tents packed wet, being later dried carefully in cool, airy conditions at home. Test for mildew even more carefully in winter; always keep the tent in its waterproof bag. Simple tears can be repaired with adhesive tape, flesh colour, used both sides of the fabric and cold-ironed in place.

A mixed grill is a main meal favourite at Scout troop camps, cooked in a large frying pan on embers.

Pegs, rubber ring guyline tensioners and spare nylon cord are best kept in a waterproof wallet and checked against loss or damage after every camp. In winter, rub a little white vaseline over all metal pegs or *pitons*, and all metal runners on guylines, as an extra precaution against damp.

It is important to choose the right tent for the job; in hill camping the fabric *must* be able to stand up to the extra, often severe wind stress; learn to pitch and strike camp in darkness if need be, and know when it is wiser to bivouac for the time being with groundsheet shelters.

A canoeist or small boat enthusiast, who is an angler, will require a long, fairly narrow tent for his gear and rod; such wedge tents are 2·3 to 3 metres long. Artist-campers find A-poles give much more space in a tent for their easels and equipment; this applies to all campers whose hobbies require an assortment of gear and tools.

Organising camp food

Sound, well-prepared food provides the fuel that gives lots of energy and zest for any programme of activity. Food must be kept separate from all other things: clothing, tentage and hobby materials especially. Never carry too much food; carry basic foods for, say, two meals, but rely on regular supplies of fresh meat, salads, vegetables, eggs, cheese and fish when possible, being available

Sample Menu for Camp

Breakfast: Muesli or uncooked porridge oats with brown sugar and hot milk. Boiled egg; crispbreads; margarine; marmalade/honey.

Mid-morning: Dried fruit; water.

Midday meal: Soup with roll (fruit juice in hot weather). Open sandwiches: hard cheese with pickle. Fresh fruit/ice cream/chocolate. Water. (*Alternatives:* cold baked beans/salad; sardines/tomatoes; canned herrings or pilchards/potato salad; Spanish omelette, hot or cold, in wedges.)

Mid-afternoon: Tea and cake.

Evening meal: 30% protein, 20% fats, 50% carbohydrates. Suggested: Pâté or eggs mayonnaise. Meat, fish or chicken with a green vegetable; potatoes or rice. Sweet or cheese, or both.

Last thing at night: Hot cocoa/meat extract in milk; chocolate.

Small polythene containers and lots of plastic bags in assorted sizes keep food tidy, and stop the fly menace; fresh meat and fish need to be eaten quickly or foxes and squirrels will show a keen interest in it!

Basic camp food plan

Balanced camp menus are best. The American Scout method has many advocates; a boy or girl needs 14 servings of food each day in camp, where 25 per cent more food is eaten than at home! Plan this so that the food intake is:

4 mugs (·85 litre) from the milk group (milk, soft cheese, soup, puddings, ice cream)

Cooking flapjacks for breakfast at a patrol camp of the 64th Nottingham Scout group.

locally or through farms. The travelling grocers in country areas, who sell almost anything, are invaluable to campers; they will also, by arrangement, leave suitable foods at cache points. I had a cache arrangement with such a grocer in North Wales, who left canned foods, flour and sugar in plastic bags, all in a wooden box hidden and protected by boulders behind a wall on a lonely mountain road. We collected the food and left notes for more requirements two days later.

2 servings from the meat group (meat, eggs, fish, chicken, meat stews, beans, peanut butter, hard cheese)

4 servings from the green/yellow vegetables and fruit group (include 1 citrus fruit and 1 tomato daily)

4 servings from the carbohydrate group (wholemeal bread, if possible, potatoes, root vegetables, cereals, rice, pasta)

Jam, marmalade and honey are not included but provide extra energy. Final choice of foods within this basic plan must depend on funds available. The plan works well both for individuals and camping units.

Cooking your food

The days of large, wasteful wood fires have gone. Today, the need is for cooking methods that do not cause conservation problems. Camp cooking fires can result in damage to wide areas of grassland, valuable as fodder and as the home of countless small creatures with a part to play in Nature's endless cycle. Wherever timber supplies are scarce, wood fires should never be used; where upland pastures are

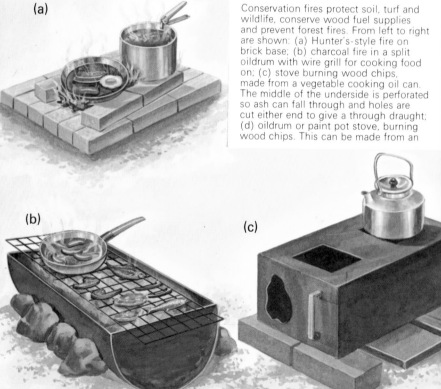

(a)

(b)

(c)

Conservation fires protect soil, turf and wildlife, conserve wood fuel supplies and prevent forest fires. From left to right are shown: (a) Hunter's-style fire on brick base; (b) charcoal fire in a split oildrum with wire grill for cooking food on; (c) stove burning wood chips, made from a vegetable cooking oil can. The middle of the underside is perforated so ash can fall through and holes are cut either end to give a through draught; (d) oildrum or paint pot stove, burning wood chips. This can be made from an also scarce, and were hard-won by farmers in hill reclamation schemes, then turves must not be removed for campers' fireplaces. It is better to rely on pressure stoves in carefully chosen, sheltered places where no risk of dangerous hill fires can result. Cooking by pressure stoves or Camping Gaz is, in any case, more efficient than wood-fire cooking.

There is nothing, however, to match the magic appeal of wood fires, and wood-fire cooking, in the open air. If mature or dead wood is available and abundant, it is good conservation practice to use it so

that healthy new growth can take its place. Cooking on fires of hot wood embers produces excellent meals, though washing-up is messier. The essential point is to ensure that sparks do not set tents on fire or cause forest fires.

Camping clubs and conduct

Camping skills improve all the time; keep up-to-date with all the developments in tent design and also

oildrum, paint pot or large fruit or jam tin, depending on size required. Holes should be punched all round for draught; (e) Scout reflector cooking fire made from an oildrum. The closer the two sections are placed, the greater the heat reflection and the faster the cooking; (f) reflector cooking stove made from a large biscuit tin placed so that it faces the camp fire. Cooking is by reflection from the polished metal of the back, sides and top of the tin as much as by direct heat from the fire.

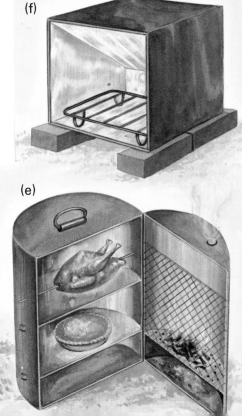

(f)

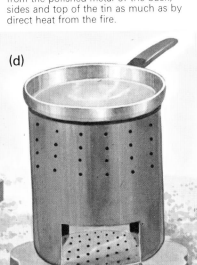

(d)

(e)

Camping by Sty Head Tarn in Cumbria.

Scout or Guide in the local community, it is wise to join a club; for example, young people in Britain can join the Camping Club of Great Britain. This friendly club caters for mobile campers of all ages and has a world-wide reputation for integrity and efficiency. Links with continental camping are close and family membership is encouraged. Its scope includes facilities for cycle, canoe and mountain camping. Photography, folk song and dance, sketching and painting are some of the special interests encouraged.

in clothing and equipment. Study the technique and gear of other campers, especially at sites abroad where so many ideas and experiences can be discussed with campers from other countries. Unless a boy or girl wishes to become a

Camping Club standards, like those of the Scout and Guide movements, are high. Members are pro-

The shelter tent can be adapted in many ingenious ways. Basically a three-metre square of waterproof canvas with strong tapes attached, it can be used, for example, as a lean-to, bivouac, sun awning or cycle shelter.

vided with full details of Camping Club sites in all parts of Britain and the Continent and information about the International Camping Carnet, essential for the Continent. The carnet permits the holder to camp at all organised sites, often at reduced charges, and includes third party insurance so that holders are covered in case of accidents or damage to property while camping.

Camping can still be enjoyed on an individual basis in Britain, on many private sites on farms by the sea in Wales and Scotland especially. Many farms provide stand pipes for water supplies, and facilities for drying wet clothes after summer storms. Showers may be available at some farms and farmers' wives will still provide a cooked evening meal, by arrangement, for campers who have been out all day on some exciting project. This facility is known in the Lake district, North Wales and the west coast of Scotland, including the islands of Skye and Mull.

It is always *essential* to have the permission of landowners' agents, the Forestry Commission or farmers who may provide a site, often with wood supplies if required. Be meticulous in securing this.

Lastly, show appreciation to a farmer host for the use of a good site, even when fees have been paid, by some good turn. Helping with the harvest, clearing scrub, repairing fences or building a bridge over a gully with railway sleepers are ideas.

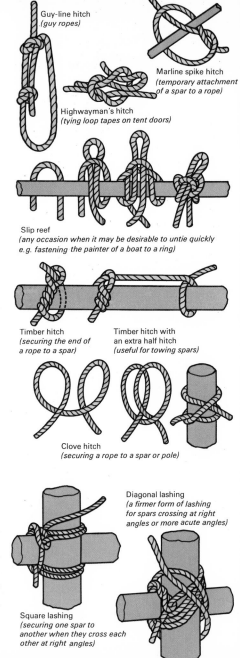

Guy-line hitch
(guy ropes)

Marline spike hitch
(temporary attachment of a spar to a rope)

Highwayman's hitch
(tying loop tapes on tent doors)

Slip reef
(any occasion when it may be desirable to untie quickly e.g. fastening the painter of a boat to a ring)

Timber hitch
(securing the end of a rope to a spar)

Timber hitch with an extra half hitch
(useful for towing spars)

Clove hitch
(securing a rope to a spar or pole)

Diagonal lashing
(a firmer form of lashing for spars crossing at right angles or more acute angles)

Square lashing
(securing one spar to another when they cross each other at right angles)

Sports

The main purpose of sport is enjoyment. It brings a sense of achievement as skill and performance improve. But it also brings other things. If we train and play hard, we become fitter. There is a Latin phrase '*mens sana in corpore sano*' (a sound mind in a sound body), which expresses the fact that if your body is fit your brain will work better, too.

Different sports require different methods of training, but exercises will help you improve your fitness. Two are shown here. In the first, lie on your back, with knees bent and hands on the floor behind your shoulders. Slowly push the body as high in the air as possible, as shown. Hold the position for two or three seconds and lower the body again. Increase the number of times you raise the body each session until you can do it 10 times. The second exercise is trunk circling. Start with feet astride and, bending forward with

arms stiff, clasp the hands together just above the ground. Describe a circle with the hands, slowly pushing as far to the right as possible, then bringing them over the head, bending backwards as far as possible, then pushing them as far to the left as possible (as shown) then slowly back to the beginning again. Practise until you can do it 10 times running. Both exercises help you remain flexible, and the fitter you are, the more you will enjoy your sport.

The sections that follow will not teach you to be a top sportsman, but they will outline the possibilities and give you some idea of what is involved in a particular sport.

Two exercises for improving fitness.

Angling

In many countries, more people practise angling than any other sport. Angling is usually divided into three main categories: freshwater fishing, sea fishing and game fishing, which is fishing with flies for such fish as salmon or trout. A fourth category might be added: sport fishing, which is the fishing for 'big game' fish such as shark or marlin.

Freshwater fishing

Since nearly everybody lives within reach of a stretch of fresh water, be it a stream, river, reservoir, gravel pit or lake, freshwater fishing is by far the most popular.

Tackle

A fully equipped angler will need rods, reels, lines, hooks, floats, leads, bait and nets. He will also need appropriate clothing and many accessories, such as a rod rest, swim feeder, seat basket and disgorger for removing difficult hooks. Add to these a rod holdall, a box for bait, a fishing bag, boots and leggings and it will be seen that a keen angler could easily spend a lot of money on his gear. It is better to spend a little more and buy good equipment than to buy the cheapest. Build up your

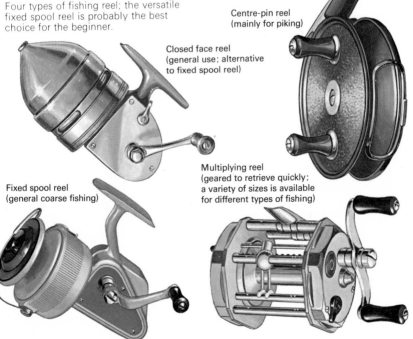

Four types of fishing reel; the versatile fixed spool reel is probably the best choice for the beginner.

Centre-pin reel
(mainly for piking)

Closed face reel
(general use; alternative
to fixed spool reel)

Fixed spool reel
(general coarse fishing)

Multiplying reel
(geared to retrieve quickly;
a variety of sizes is available
for different types of fishing)

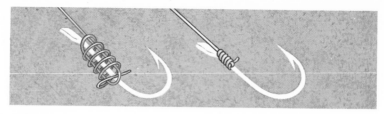

Hooks have spade or eyed ends. This shows how line is attached to a spade hook.

stock of tackle gradually, buying the best you can afford, rather than attempting to buy everything at once.

Rods should be chosen to suit yourself. Be happy with the length and weight. It would be silly for a boy to buy a rod that was too heavy for him to fish with in comfort. A light, hollow glass rod might be the best to start with, and a heavier glass or built cane rod for legering might be the second in the collection.

A fixed spool reel is simple to use and probably the best choice for the beginner – indeed, one could fish for

Floats are made in many shapes and sizes, and a selection of the most popular ones is shown below.

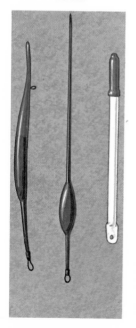
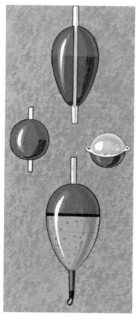
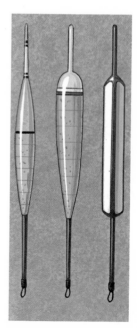

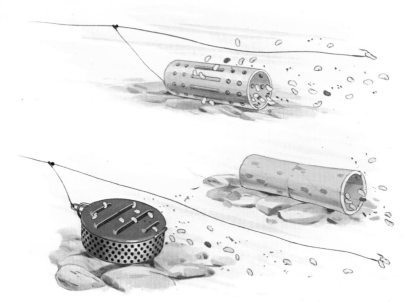

A selection of swim feeders for groundbaiting; the food attracts and concentrates the fish as it is washed out by the current.

a whole lifetime without using any other. A closed face reel has its recovery mechanism enclosed in a housing with the advantage of press button control, but some anglers do not like this. A multiplying reel is used mainly when fishing with live and dead baits or heavy lures. The centre pin reel is preferred by some for the close contact with the fish that comes of fishing from boats.

Monofilament line is the best and the beginner should buy line of say, 1 to 3·5 kg breaking strain. With a fixed spool reel the line should be loaded to within about two or three millimetres of the rim of the spool. Spools are often sold with too great

a line capacity and they should be built up with string before the line is wound on.

Hooks come in various shapes and sizes, with a spade or eyed end for whipping the line to them. Hooks are numbered by size, and a useful selection for the beginner would be from size 16 (small) to 8 (large). The line is attached to a spade hook as shown in the illustration at the top of page 104. With an eyed hook the line would pass through the eye.

A selection of floats will be required and some popular ones are illustrated. The main consideration when choosing a float is that it will cock, or stand upright, immediately after being cast. Lead shot is sometimes required between the float and the hook, particularly in running water, to make the float cock.

Methods

There are many methods of freshwater fishing, to suit the fish being caught, the type of water and the angler's preferences. The notes here will outline one or two possibilities.

The water being fished is called the swim. Sometimes it is necessary to prepare the swim by groundbaiting, which means providing food for the fish to attract and concentrate them and get them used to the food which you will use as bait. There are various methods of groundbaiting, and some are shown on page 105.

Float fishing is probably the most popular method of fishing, with the float on the top of the water indicating when a fish has taken the baited hook. Legering is a method of fishing without a float, suitable for fast water. The bait is offered on the bottom, with a single large lead weight used on the line. The rolling leger is illustrated here. Learn the techniques from books and magazines, and good fishing!

Above: The rolling leger is suitable for use in fast water. When cast across the current, the weight will travel in an arc downstream searching the swim for fish

Below: Detail of the rolling leger showing the single, large lead weight.

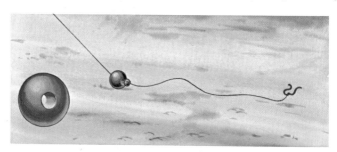

Fly fishing

Fly fishing is the usual method of fishing for game fish, such as salmon and trout. It can also be used for certain coarse fish such as perch.

There are two kinds – dry fly and wet fly. In dry-fly fishing, the artificial fly is cast on the surface of the water to look like a real fly alighting and it remains floating. In wet-fly fishing the fly sinks beneath the surface to look like a swimming insect or grub. There are many skills attached to fly fishing. Not least is the art of casting, which is throwing the line and fly on to the water. A good tackle dealer will advise on the best rods, and the casting is best learned from a teacher or by watching an expert. It is then a question of practice!

There is considerable satisfaction in making your own flies. Here again much skill is required and it is best learned direct from an expert. Some flies are direct imitations of actual insects, others attract fish although they are not copies of living insects. There are dozens of accepted patterns, many with beautiful names such as 'Red Quill', 'Soldier Palmer', and 'Silver Sedge'. They are made from such materials as wool and feathers.

Fly fishing and tying, if learned well, will provide satisfaction for a lifetime.

Casting a fly from a boat towards rushes.

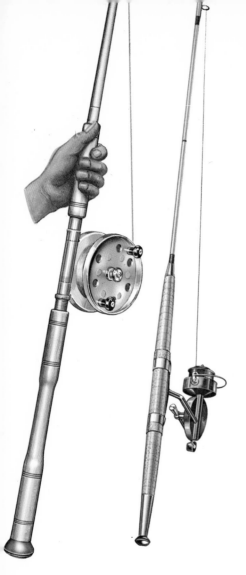

A hollow glass boat rod and single reel suitable for turbot, and (right) a light rod for plaice.

Sea fishing

Sea fishing provides plenty of variety, as it can be practised from a pier, estuary, beach or rocks, or from a boat.

Rods are usually made of fibreglass, and vary with the type of fishing.

There are two main types of reel – a large fixed spool and a multiplier. The fixed spool reel is used for casting from the shore, although it cannot achieve the distances of a multiplier. For this reason, most sea fishing experts choose a multiplying reel.

Monofilament nylon is the best line to use for spinning and shore casting, but for boat fishing a braided synthetic line is best.

Sea fishing is a pastime enjoyed by groups, and it is a good idea to join a club. This will also help you with choosing tackle, as the more expert fishermen at the club will be glad to offer advice. Your local dealer, too, will give you advice if you tell him the type of fishing you want to do.

Pier fishing

Most sea anglers begin by fishing from a pier. It has the advantage for the beginner that there will usually be other anglers to talk to and learn from.

You can usually fish from more than one level on a pier, and can choose a likely place for fish. For instance, where the piles of the pier are covered in weed there are likely to be small fish, which when caught

Above: A typical four-metre dinghy for bay fishing.
Left: Rods and reels for beach casting and for fishing in bays.

will provide bait for larger fish, such as bass or pollack. Choose strong tackle as you will have to land the fish from among the trellis work of iron supporting the pier.

When fishing from the top of the pier, remember you will need a drop-net to bring up your fish. Do not be afraid to ask for help when necessary – all anglers love to see a fish brought up.

Fishing from sandbanks

The sea around sandbanks is a good hunting ground for flat fish such as plaice, turbot and brill. The best bait is that found naturally, such as sand eels for turbot, lugworms and ragworms for plaice. Shrimps, mussels and pieces of fish are also good baits. Find a place where the food is plentiful and the fish can feed safely and easily.

Plaice can be caught from a boat inshore, and a good method is illustrated. A light rod is used, with a 2·7 kg line and very light leads.

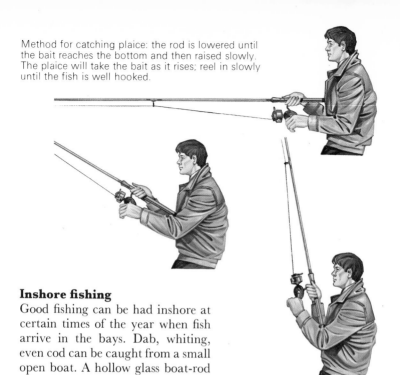

Method for catching plaice: the rod is lowered until the bait reaches the bottom and then raised slowly. The plaice will take the bait as it rises; reel in slowly until the fish is well hooked.

Inshore fishing

Good fishing can be had inshore at certain times of the year when fish arrive in the bays. Dab, whiting, even cod can be caught from a small open boat. A hollow glass boat-rod with a single action reel is capable of handling quite large fish. Use heavy line of about 16 kg breaking strain with fish bait or lugworm, but if you expect a big fish, make sure the bait is substantial enough.

Estuary fishing

Estuaries, where food is being moved in and out and around on the tide, are feeding grounds for many

A strong six-metre dinghy for inshore fishing.

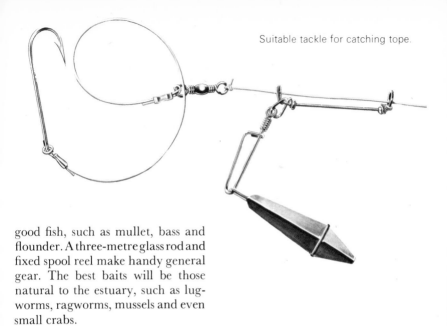

good fish, such as mullet, bass and flounder. A three-metre glass rod and fixed spool reel make handy general gear. The best baits will be those natural to the estuary, such as lugworms, ragworms, mussels and even small crabs.

Fishing for tope

Shark fishing often has an attraction for the novice angler, and tope are small sharks. They feed on such fish as mackerel, herring and flounders, and can often be caught in the neighbourhood of tide races from a boat at anchor. They run rather than dive and can be caught with a light boat-rod, a multiplying reel and plenty of line of around 30 lb breaking strain. A large strong hook and light tackle is needed. A whole mackerel, or a large fillet, is good bait. The tope will take the bait lightly and run – fast. After a pause, it will begin a second, slower run, when the angler must strike. Good sport will develop as the tope makes several runs, and the angler must be patient and not try to interrupt the

run or bring the fish to the boat too quickly.

Go tope fishing first with an expert, who can bring the tope on board and return it to the sea unharmed.

General

Sea fishing is extremely complicated. Find out the peculiarities of the coastline you intend to fish. Discover which fish are there and when. Ask advice on how they are caught and with what tackle. As mentioned earlier, the best policy is to join a club and talk to as many fishermen as possible. And remember – the sea is notoriously dangerous, even when it looks placid. Learn to swim before you think of sea fishing – and at all times take care.

Archery

Archery is an Olympic sport with its world championships, and it has the attraction that it can be enjoyed by people of all ages. Many young people make bows from yew branches and shoot sticks as arrows, but if you do this, remember that a stick can put out an eye, and never shoot if somebody is in front of you, within your range.

The best way of taking up archery is to join a club. A good archery club will run courses for beginners and its members will give you advice on acquiring the equipment best suited to your needs.

Archery has its own terminology and the parts of a bow and arrow have their special names. Some parts of an arrow are illustrated. A championship target, often made of basketwork, has concentric rings, and the scoring is 1 for an arrow in the white, 3 for black, 5 for blue, 7 for red and 9 for gold. The illustration also gives the position of the feet when shooting. The positions of the hands, and the techniques of sighting and drawing the bow are best learned by instruction from an expert, so if archery interests you, join a club where you will be welcomed and taught to become an archer.

The illustration shows a championship target, an arrow and the correct position of the feet for shooting.

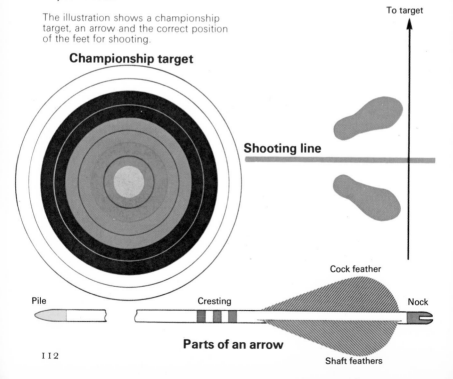

Championship target

To target

Shooting line

Cock feather

Pile

Cresting

Nock

Parts of an arrow

Shaft feathers

Athletics

Athletics can be the loneliest of sports. Although competitors may be numerous at meetings, the training is often performed alone, and can be a test of the athlete's willpower.

Broadly, athletics can be divided into track events, which include running and hurdling, and field events, which include the throwing and jumping events. Outside these categories come the marathon and walking events, and the decathlon for men and pentathlon for women, both of which include combinations of these events.

An international athlete is likely to have his own coach to map out his training schedules for him. The novice athlete can help himself by improving his general fitness and by using a training routine suited to his particular event.

Fitness

Whatever his or her event, qualities which will help the athlete are: strength, skill, stamina, speed and flexibility (or suppleness). Various exercises have been devised for each (two for flexibility are outlined on page 102), and the serious athlete will obtain a manual which details exercises for specific athletic events. Two other aids to fitness should not be overlooked. First, the athlete must eat properly. Meals should be regular and balanced, with a good percentage of proteins (meat, fish, eggs, cheese, milk) and must not be deficient in vitamins (fresh fruit and

The 110-metre hurdle event at the Montreal Olympic Games; notice how the athletes take the hurdles in their stride and tuck their knees right up to clear the barrier.

Geoff Capes puts the shot.

green vegetables are good foods). Sugar and starchy foods may be taken before competition. Secondly, the athlete must get adequate sleep in a well ventilated room.

Sprinting

Novice sprinters can help themselves with a routine which mixes bursts of flat out running with short rests in between, jogging over longer distances and weight training, since strength is an asset for a sprinter. He can also practise starting from blocks, but here it is preferable to have a coach to spot weaknesses in technique. Essentials of good sprinting are powerful drives with leg and arm, the rear leg being fully extended, and the front knee having a good lift to give a wide split between the thighs. The sprinter at speed should be relaxed – tenseness will slow him down.

Distance running

Distance runners need to do plenty of work to build up their fitness. In order to retain their enthusiasm they should vary their routine as much as possible. Days of hard training can be mixed with days of light training, days of distance running with days of jogging or sprinting in bursts. The main training will be long-distance running, with the distance being gradually increased. Changing the route periodically will avoid drudgery and staleness. With a good amount of running behind you, you will be confident that you will not be distressed during a race. Cultivate a relaxed style.

Hurdling

Study pictures of the top hurdlers for technique, and practise both for speed and for ease in clearing the hurdles. The secret of good hurdling is to be able to take the hurdles without interrupting your stride pattern. The front knee comes up hard and fast towards the chest. The hurdle is

A relaxed style is essential in distance running.

Dwight Stones, high jump record-holder, shows his technique for clearing the bar.

just cleared with the rear leg providing drive and the rear knee coming across high and fast. Think of crossing the hurdle horizontally rather than leaping upwards. As the hurdle is cleared, the front leg provides the drive for the running stride. Aim at smoothness. There should be no hesitation or checking.

Throwing

Throwing requires strength and skill – the skill to release the javelin, shot, hammer or discus at the greatest speed. Good throwers are fast, strong and supple, so sprinting practice, weight-lifting practice and flexibility exercises will all help the thrower. The best technique can be learned from a coach or by watching the champions, and it is then a question of practice and more practice.

Jumping

Good jumping comes from constant practice. The jumper should concentrate on the techniques of jumping and of his approach run. Speed and control in the run-up are essential to the jumper. The jumper should learn absolute concentration and should try to achieve control over all aspects of his sport.

Athletics clubs

If you think you have the makings of a good athlete and are prepared to devote the time and effort necessary to achieve a high standard, it is advisable to join an athletics club, where you will find others of a similar mind, facilities for training and experienced athletes and coaches to help you.

Canoeing

A canoe is a light, narrow boat, often canvas-covered, which is propelled by paddles rather than oars. Canoes have been used for sport and recreation since 1865, when John Mac-Gregor, designer of the Rob Roy canoe, wrote about his adventures on the great network of European waterways. Nowadays, there are canoeing events in the Olympic Games. Competition takes the form of racing or slalom canoeing over difficult courses containing boulders or gates, waves and conflicting currents.

The chief recreational use of canoes, apart from messing about or day runs, is touring, either inland or coastal. Combined with camping, touring can provide the adventurous with an exciting holiday.

The aspiring canoeist should learn the basic techniques from somebody who is already an expert. One of the earliest tricks to learn is

Turning the canoe using a sweep stroke.

Entering from the bank.

how to get into the canoe. The lower illustration shows how to enter from the bank. Hold on to some grass or foliage with one hand, and hold the front of the cockpit with the other. Place your nearest foot in the centre of the boat, then the other foot behind it. Keep your hands on the bank and on the front of the cockpit as you lower yourself slowly into the seat.

The illustration above shows a technique of turning the boat, known as a sweep stroke, which is used when the boat is stationary or moving slowly. Use a long forward stroke on one side and a long backward stroke on the other.

Learn from an expert, avoid weirs, use your common sense, and don't canoe if you cannot swim.

Cricket

Cricket is a team game where individuality has its greatest recognition. People talk of this player's off-drive or that player's bowling action, yet there are certain basic techniques which all great players have, and whatever the style of the young player, his game will be improved by studying them.

Batting

Even test match players exhibit a variety of stances and grips, but the young player should note that if the hands are far apart on the bat handle they cannot operate smoothly as a single unit; leverage is reduced and the freedom of swing is restricted. Practise with the hands close together near the top of the handle. The stance should be relaxed and comfortable, with the weight distributed on both feet. Ideally, the shoulders should be in a line pointing towards the bowler, from which position shots can be played all round the wicket.

Good batsmen make no unnecessary movement and move smoothly into the shot they have decided to play. Beginners sometimes get confused with advice about when to decide on the shot. Of course there is not time to debate with yourself while the ball is in flight, so it is best to practise all the shots until you can instinctively play the correct shot for any delivery.

Tony Greig follows through after completing an off-drive.

Defensive shots are played with bat vertical (called 'keeping a straight bat'). The forward defensive stroke is played with the front leg pushed forward close to the pitch of the ball, with the head well forward over the ball and the bat sloping backwards to push the ball into the ground, avoiding a catch. The back stroke is played when you cannot reach the pitch of the ball.

Gary Sobers attacks a short pitched delivery by cutting the ball through the gully.

The back foot is moved back towards the wicket and as the weight is transferred to it, the bat is brought up to stun the ball. The bat is kept straight and close to the body, with the left shoulder and elbow (of a right-handed batsman) high.

Forward attacking shots, the drives, are played like the defensive shot except that instead of the bat being held loosely to stun the ball, it is gripped firmly, and with plenty of backlift is swung through to meet the ball just after or just before it pitches. Attacking shots off the back foot, such as the cut, pull or hook, are played to short pitched balls with a cross-bat. The cut sends the

English fast bowler, John Snow.

Australian, Dennis Lillee, in the nets.

Alan Knott keeping wicket.

ball through the arc between point and wicket-keeper. The hook is played by moving the back leg to the off across the line of flight to hook the ball to leg.

Bowling

Bowlers rely on speed, swerve or spin to dismiss the batsman. All should practise length and direction. The bowling run-up and action should be smooth, not jerky, and the ball should be released from the highest point that the hand can reach. A fast bowler should aim to pitch about 5·5 metres from the batsman's wicket, a medium pacer about 4·5 metres and a slow bowler about 3·5 metres. Each ball need not be straight at the wicket. A fast bowler may want to bowl just outside the off stump, to provoke the snick to the slips. The main art is to be able to control both the length and direction of your deliveries; a good way to improve is to place a handkerchief on the pitch and to keep practising until you can pitch the ball on it nearly every time.

Leg breaks move towards the off after pitching, and off breaks break towards leg. The break is imparted by the way the ball is gripped by fingers and hand. Swerve is helped by the shine on the ball, and is consequently best delivered with the new ball. The atmosphere helps, too, the ball swinging better on a sultry day than on a clear day. Swing usually comes from the bowler's action, and even test match bowlers have been known to admit that they cannot always control the swerve.

Wicket-keeping

Wicket-keeping is a very specialised

Greg Chappell plays an attacking stroke.

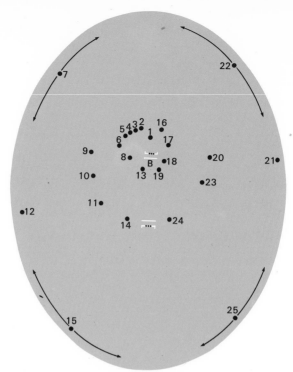

Some of the commonest fielding positions for a right-handed batsman (B)
Key: 1 wicket-keeper; 2 first slip; 3 second slip; 4 third slip; 5 fourth slip; 6 gully;
7 third man; 8 silly point; 9 point; 10 cover point; 11 extra cover; 12 deep extra cover;
13 silly mid-off; 14 mid-off; 15 long off; 16 fine leg; 17 short leg; 18 short square leg;
19 silly mid-on; 20 square leg; 21 deep square leg; 22 deep fine leg; 23 mid-wicket;
24 mid-on; 25 long on.

position and a good keeper is an invaluable asset to a side. His first job
is to make sure he is comfortable in
his equipment. He should squat just
to the offside of the wicket as the
bowler runs up and rise as he pre-
pares to take the ball. The hands
should be together, fingers pointing
downwards. Do not be afraid to
stand back to fastish bowling – when
there is little chance of a stumping,
it is best to make sure of the catches.

Fielding

Close catchers (like slips and short
legs) must be alert at all times for
the snick from the edge of the bat.
Practise short range catching with a
friend. Deep fielders should practise
taking high catches on the run and
throwing. In a match, the ball
thrown in to the wicket-keeper
should smack full toss into his gloves,
just above the stumps.

Association Football

Association football is the world's most popular team game. The finals of the World Cup might be watched on television by over 500 million people simultaneously. But playing is better than watching, as several million players of all races know.

Football is a game which currently attracts much discussion about tactics and formations. The illustrations on page 123 show how the basic playing formations have changed over the years. When modern football started just over 100 years ago, players used to follow the ball around in packs. The classical formation, which might be called 2–3–5, became standard towards the end of the 19th century, and traces of it remain, as people still talk of centre halves, even though in, say, the 4–2–4 formation there are no centre halves any more, but rather two centre backs. The illus-

trations show something of the development of formations and some of those still used today.

The young player should not bother too much about systems such as 4–2–4, 4–3–3 etc. The latest style of play, known as 'total football' assumes that all players will have sufficient all-round skills to play a fluid role, and to be able to defend, attack, pass accurately and shoot as the game demands. There is no substitute for skill, and the young player will do best to concentrate on mastering all the skills, so that he is confident in any situation and can perform any role his manager or captain might ask of him.

Ball control

A player cannot achieve anything until he can control the ball. Since the ball will come at him from all angles and at all heights, he must be able to kill it quickly with feet,

Neeskens of Holland shoots at goal.

Stanley Matthews controls the ball using his dribbling skills.

thighs, chest or head and have it under his control before he is challenged. Practise until ball control is instinctive.

The easiest way to control the ball is with the instep. Once safely under the control of your instep, you can embark on carrying the ball forward, dribbling with the inside or outside of the foot, or making a quick pass. As your ball control improves you will be able to receive the ball, turn, move off in any direction and make your next move in a continuous flowing movement. You will already be a valuable player.

Passing

Passing should be accurate. A pass to an opponent makes all your other skills useless. A good pass is constructive. It will set a team-mate free to attack. Players without the ball should be running into positions ready to accept a pass, and the good pass will take account of the receiver's run and deliver the ball just ahead of him so that he can accept the ball without checking his run. The wall-pass is a great weapon for beating opponents. Pass to a colleague and immediately run free to accept an instant 'first-time' return. The colleague is used as a wall, hence the name.

Kicking

When kicking a dead ball, as, for example, in a goal kick or free kick, beginners overlook the fact that the non-kicking foot is as important as the kicking foot. The non-kicking foot should be placed alongside the ball, and with the body over the ball the kicking foot swings through and the instep makes contact with the ball. Keep the head down, eyes on the ball, the toes pointing downwards, and follow through and the ball will go where you intend. If the

Another great footballer, Pele, passes the ball with the outside of his foot.

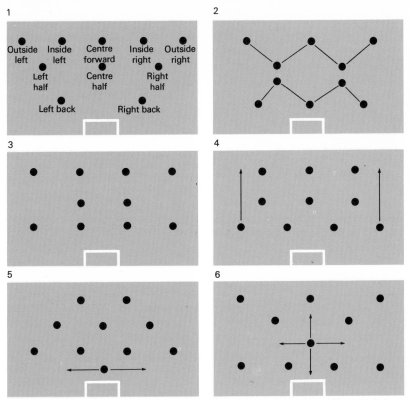

Standard formations of players. (1) classical; (2) the WM formation; (3) the 4-2-4 formation; (4) the 4-3-3 formation; (5) the *catenaccio* system with a sweeper; (6) the mid-field sweeper, as played by Beckenbauer.

non-kicking foot is behind the ball, the ball will balloon upwards.

Heading

Many goals are scored, and goal-line clearances made, with the head. If a heavy ball is headed incorrectly, it will hurt. The ball should be met with the *forehead*. The eyes can and should follow the ball until contact is made. The skull is thicker at the front, and a correct header will not hurt. The neck muscles provide the force and direction. When you have learned to head the ball correctly, you can practise jumping to meet it, and flicking it in various directions.

Tackling

Tackling wins the ball from an opponent. Unfair tackling leads to more fouls than anything else, and

Viktor, Czechoslovakian goal-keeper, attempting a difficult save.

referees have difficulty in deciding what is fair and what is not. The tackler should delay his tackle until he is sure he can get the ball, and then he should go in with speed and determination. He must keep his feet so that when he wins the ball he will be able to control and use it. Tackling is not easy to practise – skill will come from playing in as many matches as possible and learning from your own mistakes.

Goalkeeping

Goalkeeping skills are likely to be natural rather than learned. A goalkeeper needs agility, courage, anticipation and the ability to catch and hold on to the ball under pressure. If you are a goalkeeper, however, practising will not be difficult, as there will always be plenty of players willing to pepper you with shots from all angles and distances.

Franz Beckenbauer, the West German sweeper.

Johan Cruyff of Holland demonstrates ball control.

Rugby Union

Rugby Union is a game for fifteen players per side. The illustration shows the pitch and approximate positions for the players. Rugby is a very fluid game and players make different formations at line-outs, scrums and in loose play; it is impossible to be specific about positions.

The qualities required in each position are as follows: a *full-back* must be a good tackler, catcher and kicker, a *wing three-quarter* must have speed and acceleration, a *centre* must have good positional sense and be a good passer, a *fly-half* must have good tactical sense, as he, more than any other, dictates the flow of the game, a *scrum-half* must be tough, as he is frequently in the thick of the action, and he must be a good kicker and passer. Forwards are the workhorses and need strength and stamina. Forwards specialise, and a tall man may be a winner of the ball in the line-out. The *hooker* is in the centre of the front row of the scrum and must win the ball in scrums. The *Number Eight* is at the back of the scrum and must be mobile to win any loose balls.

It is impossible to describe the game in full in this article, but the principle object is to score tries by grounding the ball in the opponents' goal area. The principle methods of making progress are to run with the ball or to pass it to a team-mate. Passes must be backward.

Players should attempt to go forward, to support their team-mates and when in possession to keep the play continuous. At the same time, of course, they must prevent the opposition from doing likewise.

Positions in rugby are fluid; rough positions for the fifteen players are shown. *Key:* 15 full-back; 14 right wing three-quarter; 13 right centre three-quarter; 12 left centre three-quarter; 11 left wing three-quarter; 10 outside half or fly-half; 9 scrum-half; 8 the number eight forward; 7 right flank forward; 4 and 5 lock forwards; 6 left flank forward; 1 and 3 prop forwards; 2 hooker.

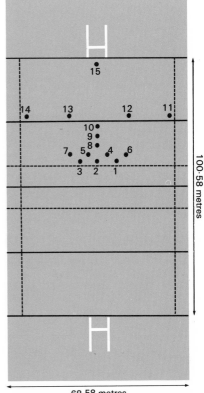

100·58 metres

68·58 metres

Unlike soccer, rugby is not easily played casually. The laws require an expert referee to interpret them. It is necessary for the keen young player to get his experience at school or with a club.

In Britain, many clubs encourage youngsters by organising mini-rugby games for boys under the age of twelve, often on Sunday mornings. Mini-rugby is for nine players a side and is played for 15 minutes each half, on a small pitch. It is the best possible introduction to the real game and a schoolboy should enquire of his local rugby clubs about the possibility of a game.

Right: A line-out is used to restart play following a kick into touch. *Below:* Gareth Edwards, in an attacking move following a scrum.

Golf

Golf is a game rarely played by youngsters, although it is taught at some schools. The difficulties a young player may face in learning the game include the expense of the equipment and the shortage of public courses. He can practise putting on a putting green, and can practise longer shots in a field with no more than a club and ball. But competition on a real course is hard to find.

A golf course consists of eighteen holes; a typical hole is illustrated. A player drives from a tee, often with a wooden club, and will then play further shots, usually with one of a range of iron clubs, until he has played the ball on to the green, when he will putt it into the hole. The object is to take as few strokes as possible, the winner in medal play being the person who takes fewest strokes for the round or rounds. Match-play golf is between two players, the winner being the one who wins most holes.

Thousands of books and articles on golf instruction have been written, and some golfers spend all their lives seeking the little extra secret that will transform them from moderate golfers into champions. A young player attempting to learn from manuals is likely to find the mass of detailed and frequently conflicting information about the positions of the shoulders, feet, hands,

Jack Nicklaus puts power into a drive.

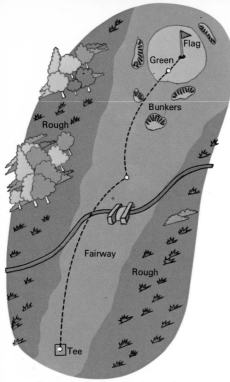

Some of the elements that make up a golf hole.

Above: Gary Player putts on the green.
Below: Severiano Ballesteros plays out of the rough.

eyes, fingers, club and practically everything else utterly bewildering.

Golf is best learned from a good coach. Most young players get their initial appetite for the game because a father or uncle plays. Perhaps he has left a club and ball around and the young player experiments and is 'hooked'. If you want to play seriously, seek advice from an adult (perhaps your school teacher) about where you can learn, or write to the secretaries of local golf clubs and ask advice about facilities for learning the game.

Hockey

Hockey is played on a pitch as shown, between two teams of eleven players, and is controlled by two umpires. The players have hockey sticks with which they try to propel a white ball into their opponents' goal. There is great skill in hitting the ball properly, as a stick is flat on one side only. The main skills lie in passing and dribbling.

There is no physical contact, and many rules are designed to avoid injury. For instance, the ball must not be hit so that it rises dangerously, and you are not allowed to raise your stick above your shoulder. If a player unintentionally puts the ball behind his goal line from within the 23-metre line, a corner is awarded to the other side to be taken from within 4·5 metres of the corner post. This is called a long corner. If the ball is put behind intentionally, a penalty corner is taken not less than 9 metres from the goal post (short corner). Attacking players must be outside the circle when a corner is

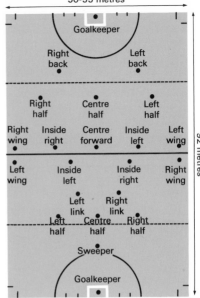

A hockey pitch; the upper formation of players is traditional, the lower one is modern.

taken and defending players must be behind the goal line.

Hockey pitches are usually less available than, say, soccer pitches, and if you are keen to take up the sport, the best way is to join a club.

Rowing, Sculling & Punting

Rowing is a general term for moving a boat through the water with oars. Sculling is a form of rowing in which one person propels a boat with two oars. Punting is propelling a flat-bottomed boat by thrusting a pole against the bottom of the river. If you are not lucky enough to own your own boat, many lakes and rivers have boathouses from which boats can be hired by the hour or day.

Rowing boats will have rowlocks, sometimes mounted on outriggers projecting from the boat, into which the oars fit. The blades of the oars are flattened into slight spoon shapes. The rowing technique is to dip the blades of the oars into the water behind you and to pull on the oars as you lean back using the oars as a lever against the water to push you along. At the end of the stroke lift the oars from the water by dipping your hands and as you lean forward, move the oars back to the starting position. As the oars move back, 'feather' them by bending your wrists upwards, so that the blades are parallel to the water.

An amusing sight is a punter who forgets to remove his pole or to let go, so that after a momentary balance on the pole he crashes into the water. If you lose control of the pole, let go. It will float, and you can paddle back with your hands to retrieve it.

Keep away from fast currents and weirs when out in a boat and (this cannot be emphasised too strongly) *never* go out boating before you can swim.

David Sturge and Henry Clay rowing in the Olympic Games coxless pairs.

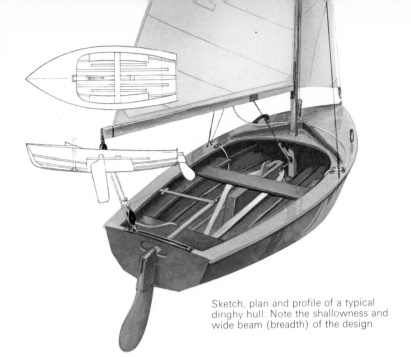

Sketch, plan and profile of a typical dinghy hull. Note the shallowness and wide beam (breadth) of the design.

Sailing

Sailing is best learned on somebody else's boat. If you have the opportunity to crew for a friend, accept it. If nobody you know owns a boat, join a club and hope that you will be asked to crew.

The cheapest of all sailing craft is the dinghy, and most beginners will start in one of these. The illustration shows a typical dinghy hull. The hull is the frame or body of a boat, without its masts, sails, rigging, etc. The front is the bow, the rear the stern. Its greatest width is its beam and its greatest depth in the water is its draught.

Other parts of a boat are as follows: the keel is the projection below the hull which helps keep the boat steady and upright; the spars are the poles which support the sails; the mast is the upright spar on which the sails are hoisted; the boom is the spar along the bottom of the mainsail; the rigging is the combination of ropes which support the mast or control the sails; the sails are the sheets which catch the wind to propel the boat.

A boat is frequently described by its rig, which is the number and position of its masts and the number and shape of its sails. The most popular dinghy rig is a sloop, and

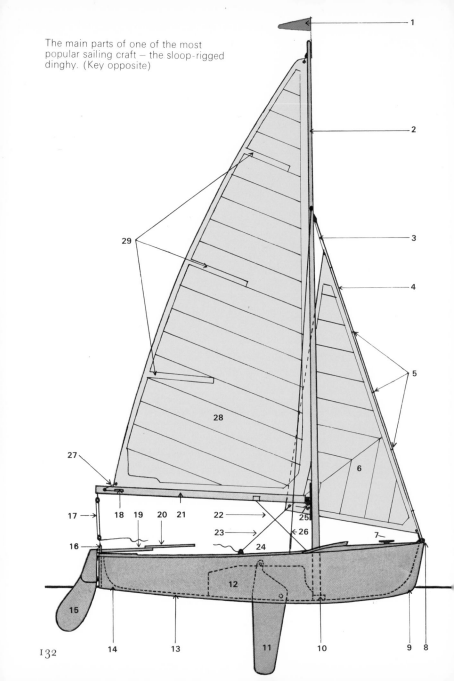

The main parts of one of the most
popular sailing craft — the sloop-rigged
dinghy. (Key opposite)

1

2

3

4

5

6

7

8

9

10

11

12

13

14

15

16

17

18

19

20

21

22

23

24

25

26

27

28

29

1 Burgee (or racing flag): indicates wind directions.	16 Mainsheet horse: metal traveller for mainsheet.
2 Mast: the main spar. Supports the sails.	17 Mainsheet: controls angle of mainsail.
3 Jib halliard: hoists jib.	18 Outhaul cleat: for securing outhaul.
4 Forestay: supports the mast (and jib) from forward.	19 Tiller: lever for steering.
5 Foresail hanks: attach luff of jib to forestay.	20 Tiller extension: increases length of tiller.
6 Jib: the single foresail characteristic of sloop rig.	21 Boom: spar along which foot of mainsail is stretched.
7 Cleat: fitting for securing rope.	22 Kicking strap: keeps the boom from lifting.
8 Bow plate: metal plate to which forestay is attached.	23 Jib sheet(s): control(s) angle of jib.
9 Stem: foremost part of hull.	24 Fairlead: alters 'lead' of sheet.
10 Mast step: takes heel of mast.	25 Gooseneck: attaches mainsail boom to mast.
11 Centreboard: retractable keel.	26 Shroud(s): lateral support(s) for mast.
12 Centreboard case (or trunk): housing for centreboard.	27 Outhaul: stretches foot of mainsail.
13 Keel: fore-and-aft centre member.	28 Mainsail: the other sail-component of sloop rig.
14 Knee: strengthening member.	29 Battens: support mainsail leech.
15 Rudder: alters direction of boat.	

this illustration showing the main parts of a sailing boat is of a sloop-rigged dinghy.

Although a boat cannot sail without wind and cannot sail directly against the wind, the boat can be made to travel in any general direction irrespective of the wind. When the wind blows from astern, the boat is travelling with the wind and is said to be *running*. When the wind is broadside on, the point of sail is across the wind, and the boat is *reaching*. With the wind blowing from ahead, the boat is travelling against the wind, and is *beating*.

Dinghy sailors must always wear life-jackets.

Never overload a dinghy tender.

When you wish to make progress against the wind, you *tack*, which is to beat first to one side and then to the other. When the wind is blowing from the port side, the boat is on a port tack. The opposite tack is the starboard tack. The boat therefore travels against the wind on a zig-zag course.

Sailing is a difficult art and the beginner (and the expert) should always think about safety. Always

The three points of sailing: when a boat has the wind astern, it is said to be running (top); with the wind on the beam it is reaching (middle); and when the boat is heading into the wind, it is beating (bottom).

wear a life jacket. Make sure that the boat is sound. If the dinghy capsizes, stay with it until help comes. You cannot learn all you need to know about navigation and weather at once, so know your limits and never attempt too much.

Skating

Many children know the pleasures of roller skating, and it is never too soon to try ice-skating. Ice-skating these days is not confined to frozen winter ponds (indeed, these can be dangerous, so do not venture on them without an adult present). Indoor ice rinks are quite widespread, and equipment can be hired at most of them. Start by hiring equipment to get the feel of the sport. The essential equipment is boots, skates and skate guards. Boots and skates can be obtained as a set. Skate guards are to protect the blades while you're not actually on the ice.

The illustrations show the set of boot and blade, views of the blade, and the correct angle for the blades when fitted. Blades that are not ver-

Gold medallist figure skater John Curry.

tical will cause the ankles to bend. Skating can be fun in itself, and as you get better, you can try some of the movements of the great figure skaters.

Skating boot and blade.

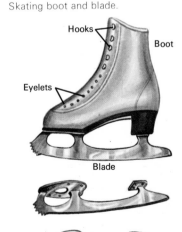

Hooks

Boot

Eyelets

Blade

Skiing

Skiing began as the best means of getting about in snow and, comparatively recently, has become a major feature of winter holidays. Skiing is nearly always learned from a qualified instructor, and all the popular ski resorts have their beginners' slopes where parties of learners are shown how to set about the sport.

Before you go for your first skiing holiday, and your first lesson, you must think about clothing and equipment. Skiing equipment consists of boots, skis and sticks. It is best for a beginner to hire these at the ski resort, as they are expensive items and you might find you do not care for the sport. In any case, a young skier will find that he soon outgrows his equipment. You should buy the correct clothes, however, such as padded ski trousers, gloves, hat, socks and sweaters. Not only must your clothes be comfortable, they must keep out the cold and be waterproof. Anoraks, balaclavas and football socks can be warm and colourful. Wear woollen or string underwear.

A skier at the winter Olympics.

Skiing uses muscles you might not have used for a while, so before you embark on your first ski holiday, obtain a book which lists some skiing exercises. You will enjoy your skiing most if you prepare for it beforehand.

Ski boot and method of releasing it from the ski.

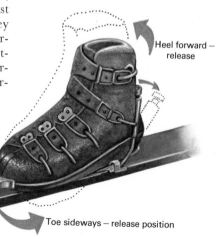

Heel forward – release

Toe sideways – release position

Swimming

The first thing to say about swimming is that it is not only a sport that gives endless pleasure in itself, it is also something that should be learned before any other sport connected with water is enjoyed.

Before you can swim, you must feel confident in the water, and the first thing to learn is how to get in.

It is best to learn with an instructor and the best place is at a swimming bath. Until you are a proficient swimmer, do your practising in a bath with an attendant present to help in case you get into any difficulties. Enter the bath at the shallow end. You can use the steps to get into the water, but the quicker and better way is illustrated. Grasping the rail which runs along the side of the bath with both hands, twist from a sitting position and slide in until the water covers your shoulders. Keep hold of the rail and stand in the water. Having got used to being in the water, you can practise dipping your face into the water (you can practise this in the bath at home), then practise taking water into the mouth (without swallowing it) and keeping your eyes open while submerging your face. The next stage is to walk in the water. Holding the rail with one hand, walk slowly from the shallow end towards the deeper end. When you have the feel of walking along the edges, you can let go of the rail to cut a corner of the shallow end. Do not be anxious and hurry. You will now be ready to try lying on the water. Holding the rail with one hand, place the other flat

Enter the water at the shallow end of the swimming pool by sitting on the edge and sliding in as shown.

The stages of breast stroke.

list all the stages a beginner goes through before he is ready to practise his first stroke. Most instructors prefer to teach the breast stroke first and as an appetiser, the illustrations on this page show the various movements of the breast stroke.

There are various other strokes, those recognised for competition in the Olympic Games being the free-style or crawl, the breast stroke, backstroke and butterfly. Many people learn to swim without proper instruction and can get around very well in the water and enjoy themselves without performing any of these strokes elegantly or well, but you will be a better swimmer if you learn the strokes properly from the beginning with a qualified instructor to each you. And remember that if Olympic results are anything to go by, the best swimmers are young.

There is nothing difficult about learning to swim, and once learned, like walking or riding a bicycle, it is never forgotten.

David Wilkie, Olympic breast stroker.

against the bath wall, elbow slightly bent, about 30 centimetres below the top hand. Pushing with the lower hand will raise your feet off the bottom until your body is lying on the water.

There isn't room in this article to

Tennis

When people talk of tennis, they nearly always mean lawn tennis, a comparatively new game which arose from a much older game variously called real tennis, royal tennis and court tennis. The older game is rarely played now, and this article is about lawn tennis.

Tennis is a game played on a court as illustrated below. The full width is used for games of doubles (two players per side). Singles matches are played in a narrower court, the inner sidelines marking the edges of the court.

All you need to play tennis are a racket, suitable clothing and footwear, an opponent similarly equipped, a court and a supply of tennis balls.

When buying a racket, try some practice swings in the shop before making your choice. Buy the best you can afford. Choose a well-known make, and a racket which feels comfortable and is not too heavy. A wooden frame is probably best for the beginner, and the grip should be square and as large as can be handled with comfort.

Most of the shots played in tennis (nearly all of those played by beginners) are ground shots, which are shots played after the ball has bounced. Most of these shots are played just as the ball is beginning to drop after bouncing. Swing the racket 'through' the ball in a full arc and follow through with the racket.

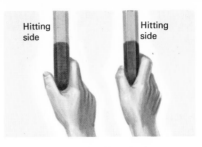

The forehand and backhand grips.

Do not stab at the ball. Both forehand and backhand shots are easy to play if you and your feet are in the right position. Getting into the right position is the most difficult part of

A tennis court.

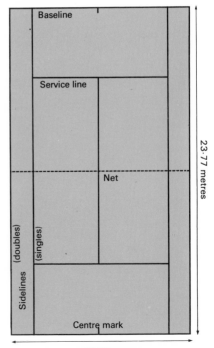

The left-handed Jimmy Connors about to hit a forehand drive.

the shot for many beginners. You can practise this art on your own by knocking a ball against a wall at various angles and speeds. Always watch the ball right on to the racket and concentrate all the time on the shot.

Each point in tennis begins with a service, so it is important to learn to serve well. As your racket is on its back swing, reach as high as you can with your 'free' hand, and try to put the ball exactly in the path of the racket as it swings through. It might help if you imagine you are throwing the racket – with practice, you should be able to serve the ball as accurately as if you were throwing it. The overhead smash shot, so necessary to world champions, is played in a similar way to the service. Throw the racket at the ball, and watch the ball right on to the racket.

Above: John Newcombe's backhand.
Below: Bjorn Borg's service.

Volleys are shots played before the ball bounces. They are played with more of a punching action than a swing of the racket and are mostly played close to the net. Ask a friend to throw balls at you at around shoulder height and jab them straight back at him.

When you can play these shots well, try lobbing and putting top spin and backspin on the ball. The best way to develop tennis skills is to find a friend willing to learn and practise with you. When you have reached a reasonable standard, you can join a club and play against other players. Do not worry too much about being beaten at first. Concentrate on your technique rather than on getting points at any price, work on your weaknesses, and eventually success will come.

Tobogganing

Most parts of the world enjoy some snow at certain times of the year and at those times, tobogganing can be great fun and cheap, too, if you can make your own toboggan.

A toboggan is basically a platform, on which you sit or lie, supported by two runners made of wood or metal. The simplest way to make one is from two planks of wood which you can curve at the front to make the runners. Join them by cross pieces to make the platform. As well as supporting the platform on top of the runners, with the fixing screws pointing downwards, put a couple of struts from runner to runner for additional support, otherwise with hard wear the runners might fold inwards or splay outwards.

All you need now is a snow-covered hill on which to toboggan downwards. Either sit upright or lie face down on the toboggan, which should be of such a length that your legs protrude at the back. Steering is done with your legs. If you are lying face down and you want to turn to your left, put your left leg out and, keeping it straight, dig it into the ground as shown in the illustration. Practise turning on a gentle slope so that you are confident of your timing and your ability to control the toboggan. Then you can tackle steeper slopes, knowing that you can avoid any obstructions.

Tobogganing is great fun but you must always be sensible and careful. Never use a slope where the snow is really icy and always allow plenty of space between yourself and any other people on the slope.

Tobogganing. The boy is using his left leg to slow down and turn left.

Water skiing

Water skiing is a sport best learned at a club with a qualified instructor. When you begin to learn, you might be surprised to find your first lessons are on shore. Your instructor may ask you to fasten on a pair of skis. While you sit upright, holding the tow rope with arms stretched before you, the instructor will pull the tow rope until you are standing in the position in which you will ski. This will get you used to the pull of the boat and perfect your stance.

Once in the water, many people learn very quickly with a good instructor. Water skiing is an exhilarating sport, and no excuses are offered for repeating this advice: learn to swim before you think of taking up this or any other type of water sport.

Below: Mike Hazelwood, British water skier, rounds a buoy on a single ski.

Above: a selection of single and double water skis.

Horses, Riding & Pony-Trekking

Learning how to look after an animal in your care is among the first considerations for any who take up riding. Some of the millions of young and old who ride today, do so, however, without taking on that responsibility; they hire their horses and ponies from riding schools and equestrian centres where the animals are cared for by the staff employed. Others, and these are the great majority, are not happy unless they are riding a horse or pony to which they have devoted time and effort in seeing that it is well cared for and well presented.

When choosing a pony, size and temperament are the important considerations. Ideally, your feet should hang a little above the girth when you are mounted, but it is sensible to choose a pony that is a little bigger than you need rather than one that is a little on the small side. Without doubt the best all-round ponies are the British native breeds, and two of these are shown opposite. However, many of the best riding ponies are not thoroughbreds, but are the result of cross-breeding: they usually have some native blood and so have many of the qualities of the native breeds.

Stable management is a complex and detailed subject since, paradoxically, not all horses and ponies are kept in stables. But, whether it is grass-kept or not, the caring of a horse or pony is crucial for its well-being. The 'management' of the grass-kept, in other words those which live outside the year round, is as important as the management required to keep a stable-kept horse fit. Many books are available which go into this subject in great detail. These will teach you some of the things you need to know, but there can be no substitute for practical experience, and the best way to learn horse and pony care is to be with them day after day.

First, let us examine the differences between a grass-kept and a

Paddocks may be divided into strips in order to conserve the available grass or if a pony needs to be confined to a small grazing area because he is too fat.

Connemara pony

Welsh Mountain pony

stable-kept animal. In winter months, a grass-kept horse will require additional or supplementary feeding to make up for the small amount of nutritious value in what-

ever grazing is available. If possible, the horse should be given good quality hay regularly, for it seldom pays to buy the cheapest fodder. In the severest of weather a treat can

A good all-round, cross-bred pony

Palomino

Yew   Laburnum   Rhododendron   Deadly nightshade

be offered in the form of a bran mash, to which can be added vitamins. During the springtime, however, when the grass is fresh and lush, there is a tendency for any horse or pony to graze contentedly throughout the day. This will help neither his shape nor condition! Over-feeding on spring grazing will, in all probability, demand a pretty firm programme of exercise and ridden work.

By their nature, ponies are demanding of company. They are not happy when left alone in a field, or when they are left because the weather is bad, or because they will not be wanted until the weekend. Regular attention *must* be given. The horse or pony's health *must* be watched. The fences around the paddock or field *must* be checked. Fresh water *must* be available. Dangerous plants *must* be removed.

The ideal area of grazing for a pony is about two acres, not a parcel of land the size of a tennis court! But two ponies could happily graze in less than four acres. All land is improved by 'resting' and it is a good idea to fence off part of the area to enable it to recover and not be overworked. Harrowing, rolling, treating and ensuring good drainage will

Grass-kept ponies should be provided with some form of shelter. If there are no trees or hedges available, a three-sided shelter, such as the one pictured, is a necessity.

Ragwort

Briony

Privet

Hemlock

Laurel   Foxglove

The wild plants and shrubs of the hedgerow are pretty to look at but some, such as those shown above, can be poisonous to horses and ponies. Paddocks should be examined carefully and any offending plants rooted out and burnt.

all help and where there is any doubt, experts, perhaps a local farmer, should be consulted.

Water for drinking should be fed into a trough with a ballcock to control the flow. Where it is not possible to supply piped water, the troughs should be filled by hand each day and they should be emptied frequently and cleansed thoroughly before refilling. Stagnant water is highly dangerous and must be avoided.

It is also important that some form of shelter or shed (see illustration on page 146) is provided for a

Three of the best types of fencing for fields used for ponies are shown below. Barbed wire fencing is not recommended.

Post and rail fencing

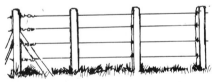

Posts with tight wire strands

Hedge

To prevent water becoming lodged in the hollow of the heel when washing a pony's feet, press the thumb of the hand holding the foot well into the hollow.

gerous weeds and plants are not beginning to grow there. Where these are spotted do not simply pull off the tops and believe that is all there is to it. Digging up and burning is the only safe procedure.

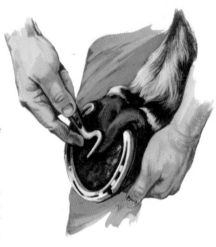

A hoof pick should always be used working downwards from heel to toe to prevent any risk of the pick penetrating the soft parts of the frog.

grass-kept pony. This should be erected at the edge of a field with its back to prevailing winds. Another job that demands close attention is the regular inspection of the land and hedgerows to ensure that dan-

So far, we have been thinking about the grass-kept horse or pony. Yet much of what has been written applies to stable-kept animals as well and will be dealt with in greater detail in the following pages. All horses and ponies, however they are stabled and kept, require a regular routine of feeding, watering and grooming. By ensuring this you will be helping to maintain their condition and well-being. .

Hoof oil improves the appearance and is beneficial to broken or brittle feet.

The Points of a Horse

1 Forelock
2 Cheek Bone
3 Nostril
4 Chin Groove
5 Throat
6 Jugular Groove
7 Shoulder
8 Breast
9 Elbow
10 Knee

11 Cannon Bone
12 Coronet
13 Heel
14 Pastern
15 Chestnut
16 Girth
17 Chest
18 Abdomen
19 Sheath
20 Shannon

21 Fetlock
22 Hoof
23 Hollow of Heel
24 Hock
25 Gaskin
26 Stifle
27 Buttock
28 Dock
29 Thigh
30 Croup

31 Haunch
32 Flank
33 Loins
34 Ribs
35 Back
36 Withers
37 Mane
38 Crest
39 Axis
40 Atlas

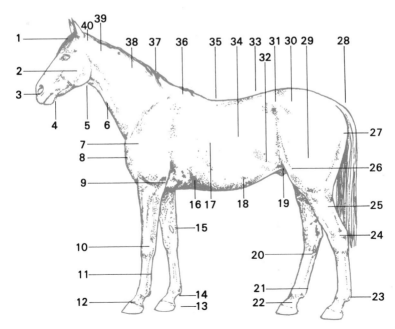

Stable management

Stable management covers a number of routine jobs, one of which, whether it is for the stable-kept or grass-kept, is the need to see there is absolute cleanliness at all times. A stable should be emptied of all bedding at regular intervals and the walls and floor hosed down and swept clean. Every day, the buckets and feeding utensils must be thoroughly cleaned before re-using.

The entire area surrounding the stable will have to be kept free from litter and dirt. Sweeping up is hard work if it is to be done properly, and it may be necessary to do this twice a day! See the 'muck heap' is tidy. Do not permit the fodder store or tack room to become disorderly or out of hand. Everything about the horse or pony, about the field or paddock, about the shelter, about the stable and stable area, about saddlery and tack, and about you, should be as clean, neat and tidy as can possibly be managed.

Different materials can be used for bedding – straw, peat, wood chips, shavings and even shredded paper. Some horses and ponies do not do well on straw, finding it is too dusty. Others may not be happy on wood chips or shavings. Whichever material is used, and there must always be a deep bed, it will require forking over each day and all the dirty or stained material should be removed.

Feeding will depend to a large extent on the type and amount of work the horse or pony is being asked to do, and its age, temperament and overall condition. The owner, or the person looking after a stable-kept horse, must decide how best to keep the animal fit and contented. Appearance is a guide for the experienced, but always be on the lookout for signs of lack of condition.

Four of the most common rugs for stable-kept horses and ponies.

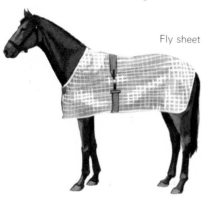

Fly sheet

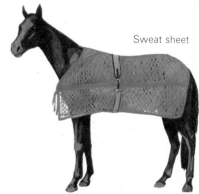

Sweat sheet

Some simple rules for good feeding are :

1 Feed little and often.

2 Water before feeding. Always see there is fresh water available in the field and stable.

3 Allow some grazing each day for the stable-kept.

4 Feed at the same time each day.

5 Do not work a horse or pony immediately after a feed.

6 Feed hay every day to stable-kept horses and ponies; feed it to grass-kept horses and ponies during the autumn and winter months.

7 Do not make sudden changes in the type of feed. If a change is necessary, introduce it gradually.

8 Always feed the best possible forage.

Night rug

Day rug

Tack

The word 'tack' embraces the equipment worn by a horse or pony. If kept in good condition this will last for years and frequently outlives the horse for which it was originally bought. Many owners and stables retain all tack and will not allow it to be sold when they part with a horse or pony. Tack rooms become full with bridles, saddles, bits, leathers and odd, miscellaneous pieces. Sometimes this can be useful, but only if the piece of tack available fits the requirement. This is most important – it must *fit*!

A saddle should never be used if it is not of the correct size, for it could bring untold damage to the horse's spine and back. It is wrong to believe one saddle will do for two or more horses, even where they stand at the same height. A saddle, like all tack, is a personal item of equipment – personal to the horse or pony for which it is bought and fitted. Just as a rider will be conscious of the danger in wearing a riding hat that is too large or too small, so must he be aware of the dangers that arise when using tack or saddlery that is not fitting as it should.

On this page we illustrate the names given to the different parts of the saddle. The girth, the means by which the saddle is held across the horse's back, can be made from leather, webbing or nylon. A girth is quite separate from the saddle and is buckled either side under the saddle flaps. It must be tightened sufficiently to hold the saddle firmly in place before the horse or pony is mounted, and will require further

The parts of a saddle.

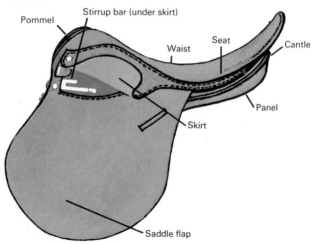

Pommel · Stirrup bar (under skirt) · Waist · Seat · Cantle · Panel · Skirt · Saddle flap

adjustment once the rider is seated in the saddle. Leathers, which hold the stirrups, are slotted into the stirrup bars.

The bridle, whether a Snaffle, Pelham or Double, is the means by which the bit is supported and held, and the bit is used to control the energy built up by correct application of the aids. Some bits are more severe than others, but even the most gentle of bits can be punishing to the bars of the horse's mouth if they are incorrectly fitted and used.

The reins should be seen as an extension of the rider's hands, used to control the horse's mouth. When contact with the bit is adjusted, usually by opening or closing of the fingers, the horse will either tighten or relax his jaw. Reins are not fitted to enable a rider to keep his balance, or to tug when he wants to turn! Remember, reins are attached to the bit, and it is the bit that relays your instructions to the horse, providing that the bars of the mouth have not lost their sensitivity through being

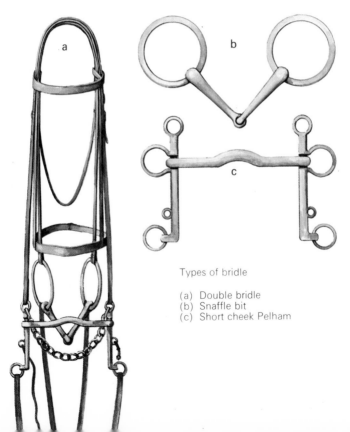

Types of bridle

(a) Double bridle
(b) Snaffle bit
(c) Short cheek Pelham

handled too roughly, and that it is used in conjunction with the other aids.

Other items coming under the heading of tack include rugs, bandages, head-collars, leading reins, martingales, tail guards, and numnahs.

Cleaning saddlery, apart from helping to preserve it, gives an opportunity to examine the stitching. Accidents so easily occur when the reins or leathers break. The saddle, too, will require attention, and it should be sent to a saddler once a year to be checked and, if necessary, re-stuffed.

When cleaning tack, each part must be unbuckled and treated separately. It is not possible to clean a saddle or bridle when it is assembled for use. Do not use very hot water or soda, as these will remove the oils in the leather and will make it brittle and liable to crack. Wash every item in warm water and wipe dry. Then apply saddle soap, which contains all the ingredients for cleaning and keeping the leather in good order.

Left: the illustrations show the way to put on a bridle and how to check that nothing is too tight.

The rider pictured opposite is sitting comfortably in a well-fitting, modern saddle that will give her the maximum amount of help in maintaining her seat. Because the saddle fits well and positions the rider centrally, it will also help the horse to give of his best.

Beginning to ride

Most sports and pastimes introduce words that make it seem as if one is learning a new language. Many of these words are traditional and, as far as riding is concerned, must be learned if one is to understand the words of instruction given and be able to follow what is written in riding manuals. Just as we have looked at the names given to different parts of a saddle, so we must learn the names or 'points' given to different parts of the horse (see illustration on page 149). These continually come up in conversation with those who ride, and are perhaps the first thing you should learn about riding.

Although there is much to know before getting on the horse's back, we will begin here by looking at mounting and dismounting. Mounting is best done from the nearside, either with the horse or pony having previously been tied up, or with his head being held by an adult or an experienced young rider. First, check that the girth is tight. Then, facing the horse's tail, take the reins firmly in the left hand. Place the left foot into the stirrup (be sure you are wearing shoes or boots with a heel) and take hold of the pommel of the saddle with the right hand. Swing

The four pictures above and opposite show the approach and the sequence of footfalls in the canter pace which is one of three-time.

round and face the side of the horse. Next, spring from the ground and pass the right leg over the quarters, making sure the horse is not kicked in the process. Finally, lower yourself gently into the saddle, place your right foot in the stirrup and take up the reins with both hands. Once again, check the girth, and correct the length of leathers if necessary.

To dismount, the reins are taken into the left hand and both feet are removed from the stirrups. With a swing, the right leg comes back over the quarters and both feet land together.

Once you have mastered the technique of mounting and dismounting, and before setting off, it is well to consider the 'aids', or the signals given by the rider to the horse or pony to let him know what he is being asked to do. There are two types of aids – the natural and

the artificial. The natural aids are applied by use of the hands, legs, body and voice. Artificial aids comprise the use of a stick or whip, spurs, martingales and so on.

To move forward, the reins are gathered until light contact is made with the horse's mouth. The rider's legs are moved slightly behind the girth and squeezed. The rider's body and body weight must be such to give him balance and a secure seat; the body is also used, with the legs, to build up and maintain impulsion – the energy that comes from behind the saddle. To keep the pace, therefore, the rider's hands keep contact with the horse's mouth, his legs keep him moving forward in the selected pace, and the body maintains the energy and balance.

In addition to using his legs in moving forward, the rider must also use them for directing and control-

ling the horse's hindquarters. When turning to the right, the rider will move his left leg further behind the girth and leave his right leg in its normal position. The hands might at this moment show a light pressure on the side to which the rider intends to turn. To turn to the left, the action of both hands and legs are reversed.

To sum up, we must look again at the words which, when understood and applied, play such an important role in riding – balance, collection and impulsion. *Balance* in a horse is when his weight and the weight of the rider are distributed to allow him to move with maximum ease and efficiency. A horse is said to be *collected* when he has control over his legs so that he can obey instantly any signal given him by the rider. He should be on a light rein and the whole of his body should be collected into a shortened form. *Impulsion* means energy; the force built up in the horse's quarters by use of the rider's legs and body.

A morning gallop across the downs. The riders are in full control of their horses, leaning slightly forward with their reins held a little further forward than usual.

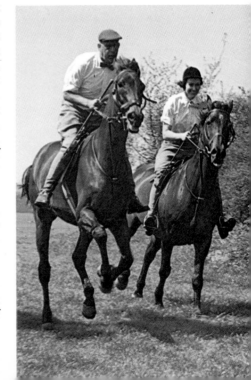

Schooling

Planned and regular schooling and exercise is necessary if a horse or pony is to be kept fit and alert. The type of exercise will depend on several factors: the age and condition of the horse or pony; whether he is grass-kept or stable-kept; the time of year and the condition of the going; and the amount of work being asked of him.

One effective form of exercise can be given when riding in a paddock or when out hacking. Use this time well. Teach the horse to halt at the place you choose. Ask him to move off with the correct leg leading. Allow him to move through the paces using the collected and extended strides. Encourage him to use his muscles. And think of yourself! Exercise and schooling must also apply to the rider.

The turn to the right showing the left hand yielding as the right acts, while the right leg is applied on the girth and the left is held behind the girth, to prevent the quarters swinging outwards.

The picture shows riders crossing a grid of poles at walk. This is the first exercise in jumping.

Walking on roads can also be of benefit to a horse, but never use the roads as you would the paddock or commons. Remember the Highway Code and be considerate at all times.

The reason for schooling is to help develop the horse or pony and to teach obedience to the rider's instructions. For example, we school a horse over cavalletti (trestle-type fences) or coloured practice fences to teach the rider to develop his riding position over jumps, combined with good balance, strength and style. We should make sure that time spent over practice obstacles will also be teaching these attributes to the horse or pony.

We school in a dressage arena to perfect suppleness and obedience. In the manège we lead the horse through a variety of movements to enable him, and his rider, to learn to 'come together' and to improve

Riding a circle is an important aspect of schooling. The pony's spine should be in line with the circumference of the circle being made.

their partnership. If they are to be successful, both horse and rider must understand and respond to one another – schooling will go a long way towards achieving this.

Schooling for jumping is more involved, though it must never be thought to be too highly technical and complicated for the novice. Practise over the poles, then move to cavalletti, the trestle-type fences constructed to give different heights for jumping by easy adjustment to the 'wings'. When the stride pattern is mastered and you feel ready to move on, small practice obstacles should be attempted. These might vary between upright and spread fences, and between parallels and ascending jumps. They can easily be

constructed, even by using bales of straw, but do not build them in an unsafe condition. Avoid using barrels, unless they lie on their sides. Check there are no protruding nails on poles, and do not construct obstacles without ensuring that each can be knocked down easily and without injury when hit.

More advanced schooling, perhaps over fences of a cross-country nature, will come later and should preferably be used in conjunction with an instructor or another person 'on the ground'. Schooling and exercise must never be boring to the horse or rider. Vary it frequently and, once you have achieved your objective in any aspect, move into another part of the routine.

Cavaletti are used for many different exercises. By placing them on top of one another you can make larger jumps and spreads as you progress. Three arrangements are shown here.

Low parallel

High jump

Spread jump

Right: A horse will judge his distance from a jump by looking at the part of the fence on or nearest to the ground. It is consequently easier if he is given a distinct ground line like a pole.

Riding holidays and pony-trekking

When you are reasonably competent in riding skill, and once you know something about looking after a horse or pony, you might like to consider riding holidays, which are now organised by a number of well-managed and well-established centres. This type of holiday is a good way to learn still more about riding and horsemanship, for the better centres spend time each day giving instruction and guidance.

Before you arrive, the centre will ask for some indication of your riding experience so that a suitable horse or pony will be ready for you to look after during your stay. You will be expected to groom, feed and generally care for 'your' pony. You will have an opportunity to meet other young people – some of whom may never have ridden before while others may be quite experienced.

Pony-trekking in the Black Mountains in Wales on a young adventure holiday.

Riding holidays are available in many parts of the British Isles, from the quieter parts of the New Forest and Dartmoor to the remoter areas of Scotland. In Wales, there are several centres catering for different types of holiday, and there is always wonderful riding to be had in Ireland.

Another form of holiday is to go pony-trekking, now popular in many parts of Europe. Trekking can take several forms: the half-day or full-day trek, where the ride begins and ends at a particular centre, or the long-distance trek, where the ride is spread over several days and there is a stop each evening with accommodation provided for both ponies and riders. A long-distance trek is really for the advanced rider, since it is almost a mounted expedition! It does not necessarily finish at the point from which it started.

Riding holidays are listed each year in features in the magazines *Horse and Hound* and *Riding*. In Scotland, there is an approved list of centres published by the Scottish Sports Council and a list is also produced by the Scottish Tourist Board. In Wales, an approach should be made to the Welsh Tourist Board. Other Associations have been formed in particular regions, and the Pony Club can also give advice on the centres approved by the British Horse Society.

A group of young people enjoy a riding holiday in a picturesque part of Somerset, England.

Outdoor Hobbies

Watching garden birds

Handicapped children, and any boy or girl recovering from illness and having to spend much time in bed, can become involved in this outdoor hobby, which is enjoyed by many fit and healthy young people. Bird-watching is a fascinating pastime requiring quiet and patience. For the person confined to bed, bird tables of several different kinds can be fixed to window sills on short wooden arms or metal brackets (see illustration below). Access will have to be made from a window for stocking the table with food, cleaning it and supplying a small non-tip pot of water for drinking and bathing.

Open tables are better than nothing, but with these the food is hogged by larger birds and the tables tend to get messy. A better idea is to have a fixed or hanging table with a cover; round ones are popular, with the cover fixed so low

Bird tables suitable for smaller birds can be fixed to window sills using metal brackets.

Nut hoppers made from plastic-covered wire netting, with sticks for perches, are popular with many birds.

made mix of peanuts, stale fruit cake, dried fruit, apple cores, which most birds love, and chicken corn, in melted beef dripping. This savoury mix sets hard and can be made in an old dish, which can be left on the table. Alternatively, put the soft mix in a piece of wire netting that has been shaped round a tennis ball, and then, when it has set hard, it can be hung on the table. Hanging metal containers with perches are also a good idea. Fill the container with peanuts, suet or bacon rinds.

on the frame that only small birds can use it. The cover will also protect the table from rain and snow. The table should have a flange to prevent food falling off and drainage holes in case water is spilled or rain gets in.

The best food in winter is a home-

Visitors to the table will include all members of the tit family, greenfinches, which grow so tame that they can be stroked as they feed, dunnocks and even ground-feeders like robins and chaffinches. The noisy starlings have to be content with the crumbs dropped below, with blackbirds and thrushes in hopeful attendance. Keep a daily log of visitors and try sketching them.

Bird tables like this one can be made easily at home and hung in the garden.

Collecting feathers

Walks in woods or parks, and on commons or seashores often produce collections of beautiful feathers, which have been discarded by birds in midsummer. Sometimes birds get involved in scraps among the branches of trees, which result in them losing feathers. I have seen feathers flying down from fights between magpies, notorious predators, and collared turtle doves protecting their eggs or young. The doves are among the most courageous fighters and I have yet to see the magpies win. Scraps may also occur in the open fields near the sea between jackdaws and gulls or lapwings. Feathers are left behind in abundance.

Collect only the best feathers, the most colourful and striking. Mount

A feather collection can be attractively displayed in a photograph album with loose-leaf pages.

them in a modern photograph album with a dark or tinted background on the pages to provide contrast. Make a brief note of the bird when the feather has been identified and add the date and place found. Feathers can be mounted with Sellotape or placed under the adhesive transparent sheets provided with some albums. The col-

Jay

Green
woodpecker

Partridge

Wood
pigeon

Pheasant (quill
and contour
feather)

Mallard

Kingfisher

lection will provide an original logbook of many pleasant hikes and exploring projects outdoors. Do not be tempted to exchange feathers with friends; it is much more interesting to collect only those you have found yourself.

Adopting a stream

Streams give endless pleasure on hikes. They can be followed for miles through woods and fields, along the foot of railway embankments, on the perimeters of golf courses and in the hills. Some of the finest streams I have found have been in the outskirts of large cities, always near railways or golf courses. Others have been high in the hills and fells of country areas.

It is great fun to adopt a stream and keep a continuous watch on it. The best plan is for a team of friends, say eight, or a patrol of Scouts or Guides to choose a certain length, perhaps two kilometres, between two obvious points. The entry point could be, for example, where the stream, which might be a surface

Adopt a length of stream between two obvious points and start by clearing debris such as dead leaves.

water drainage channel, tipples out of a culvert at the foot of a railway embankment. The exit point may be where the stream joins a small river. Buy a large-scale map of the area and mark these points clearly on it.

Acquire a large but inexpensive desk diary, the kind that has one page for every day of the year if pos-sible. Notes about the stream should be recorded daily by the team, working in twos or threes.

Mark several garden canes in centimetres. They will enable the water depth to be recorded at all seasons, something that should be done in 10 to 20 suitable places. This information is invaluable.

Record the state of conservation.

Clear debris, washed down after winter storms, which blocks the stream at vulnerable points. Systematic clearance will prevent flooding, which would cause the loss of topsoil and the natural cover and food supplies of birds and other wildlife. Record the wild bird life, nests and any information on young successfully reared and so on. Identify all birds and wild animals. Make as many notes as possible on bird and animal behaviour.

Do not divulge the sites of animal homes if found because conservation depends so much on responsible people knowing how to respect wildlife. Keep a close watch on the creatures that live in and around the stream, such as frogs, newts and sticklebacks; identify the plants growing in and near the stream and prune the unruly and overgrown ones that cause silt to accumulate and block channels. At the same time do not be too ruthless about this because plant life provides cover for small fish and water creatures, and so is vital for their survival.

In wilder places look for otters, delightful creatures which use flat rocks in mid-stream as vantage points on food swims, or in the training of young otters to seek their own food. If a holt (an otter's lair, a dry warm den under a quiet, overhanging bank) is found, then do everything to protect it.

Check regularly for pollution and vandalism. Seek adult help if the stream is being abused in any way. Within twelve months, your daily diary will make fascinating reading, especially if photographs of the before and after appearance and simple sketches are added. A great team effort!

Identify all plants and animals and keep a close watch on the creatures that live in and around the stream. Make daily notes of your observations in a diary over a twelve-month period.

Collecting coloured sands

Some years ago in North Wales, a boy who was exploring around Abergele on a holiday hike with a friend, happened to notice that the local sands of the area varied a great deal. It interested him so much that he started to collect them in small linen bags, the kind that geologists use to collect fossils and rock samples. The boy's search took him to all parts of North Wales from Chester to Anglesey. Before long, he had a fine collection of coloured sands ranging from jet black to many shades of red, yellow and white. He kept a record of all his sands, placing samples in round pillboxes with transparent, plastic lids, numbered to correspond with numbers on his maps showing where he had found the sands. Each pill-

box was also marked with the date of the find. This boy's collection was the first of its kind and it became a museum collection. As a personal field project it was a huge success.

This project led the boy on to more field work. In the Isle of Wight he found beautiful red and yellow-ochre sands around the Needles. Another collection resulted, this time displayed in sealed test tubes, as well as the boxes he had used

before. More collections followed from hikes and camps in Skye, where there are some fine beaches of coral sands, and even dazzling white sands. Anglesey provided another collection with its deep, rich red sands, much used by builders, and its lovely golden sands. The boy also extended his collection by exchanging sands by post with Scout friends in California, Sri Lanka and Australia.

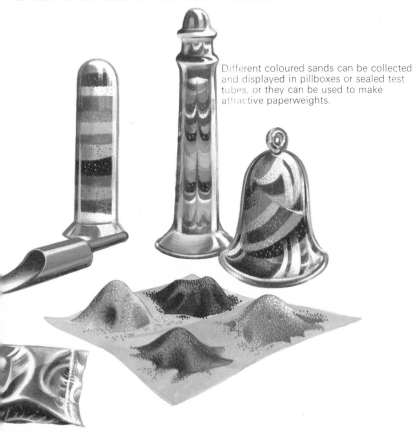

Different coloured sands can be collected and displayed in pillboxes or sealed test tubes, or they can be used to make attractive paperweights.

Collecting fossils & stones

Collecting fossils and attractively coloured stones and rocks is a natural sequel to collecting sands since so many are to be found on and near beaches, in soft cliffs and harder rocks. Much rock material can be found inland as well with every hope of finding beautiful specimens for a collection of rocks and stones. Streams and rivers expose suitable rock faces just as the sea exposes cliff faces. With personal safety ever in mind, explore the foot of inland cliffs, old quarries no longer used for building stone, mines, railway cuttings, motorway developments, and any site used for dumping rock material from deep bore-holes and wells.

Wherever rock has been exposed for one reason or another there is an opportunity to collect specimens from the exposed, undisturbed face. The equipment needed is a simple geologist's hammer with a square face on the head and chisel edge at right angles to the shaft; a trowel for softer rocks; a cold chisel; a magnifying glass, about 10 cm in diameter, a notebook, newspaper for wrapping up larger stones and plastic or cotton collecting bags.

Smooth oval stones found on shingle beaches and in rock pools left by the tide are very often worth collecting, as they can make attractive arrangements in glass bowls. The best size is that of a small potato, not too large or too small. Aim for contrast; collect together a selection of white, black, various green, grey and buff stones and if possible, a red mottled stone and a black and white mottled one. Also, for fillers, find a small selection of flat, white or coloured stones.

Scrub the stones clean of sand and

A good beach for pebble hunting.

Seashore pebbles and stones of varying shape and colour are very attractive in bowls of fresh water.

anything else using a small nail brush and plenty of cold water. Do not use soap or hot water, which seems to spoil the appearance of pebble stones. Now buy one or two round goldfish bowls, medium to large size, from the pet shop. Alternatively, you can find attractive bowls that have the glass tinted or streaked with colour.

Wash and dry the bowls. Place some of the stones carefully in the bottom, then add more stones to fill about half to two-thirds of the bowl. You may have to do this several times to get the required contrast or it may be achieved first time. Finally, cold water should be poured in until the stones are well covered with clear water.

This beautiful bowl of stones can now be placed on a window sill in a position where the sunlight, especially the stronger morning sun, will pass through it. It will remind you of happy outdoor holidays and day trips. If you wish, the water can be tinted slightly with a little red or green ink.

The bowls serve a dual purpose since they provide any room that has central heating with the humidity needed for comfort. The water disappears gradually, but it is best to renew it every ten days in winter, and at least once a week in summer, otherwise a discoloration will take place and green algae may start to grow on the side of the bowl. However, after several changes of water, the bowls lose this tendency.

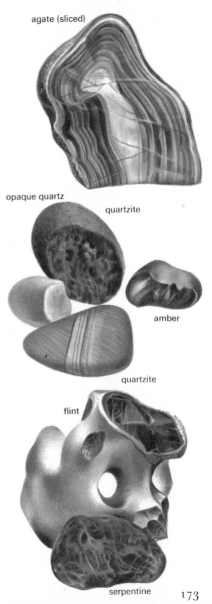

Some types of pebbles to look out for on the beach.

agate (sliced)

opaque quartz

quartzite

amber

quartzite

flint

serpentine

173

Making things with shells

Shells may be used to make attractive arrangements in bowls in the same way as I have described for stones, but they do not have the same magic as stones. However, shells make lovely paperweights if small ones are collected and packed tight into clear plastic tumbler or dish. The dish should be sealed with modelling cement placed on top of the shells and made completely flat by smoothing it over with a blunt knife. Leave the dish in a cool place until the modelling cement has hardened. If the top is flat and does not require any glasspapering to make it completely smooth, the paperweight is finished. Turn it up the other way and there it is, ready for use!

Shells have been put to many other uses, especially those found in tropical countries and in Australia. In Victorian times, photo frames, jewellery boxes and correspondence boxes were decorated on the outside with tropical shells and then varnished. Attractive necklaces have been made with small shells, and cowrie shells have been used as money! Pearl buttons have been cut from shells and large conch shells have been known to make reliable axe-heads.

Jewellery making

Many semi-precious stones can be found on beaches which, after being cut and polished, make attractive brooches or pendants. There is no chance of finding precious stones on

Shells can be used in many attractive ways such as in decorating boxes.

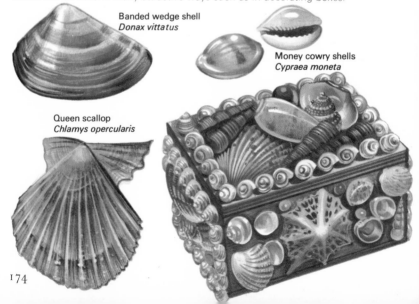

Banded wedge shell
Donax vittatus

Money cowry shells
Cypraea moneta

Queen scallop
Chlamys opercularis

a beach! There are only five kinds: diamonds, rubies, sapphires, emeralds and opals. But remember, a very good gem stone can be more valuable than a poor quality diamond. Natural stones include agate, amethyst, aquamarine, topaz, golden beryl, smoky quartz and fluorspar. These stones can be found in other places besides beaches.

A good place to start searching for gem stones are the rock falls at the base of cliff faces; comb one small likely area thoroughly and also look above all high-water marks. Agate is a striped stone of striking beauty and many colours. Agates with black and white striped bands are called onyx and those with brown and white bands, sardonyx. The Suffolk coast, where agates are found, is one of Britain's best hunt-

Making animals and flowers from shells.

ing grounds for beach jewels. Red jasper, which takes a high polish, is found at the north end around Felixstowe; you may also find amber and jet.

Honey-brown yellow amber from

This selection of beach pebbles has been polished in a pebble tumbler.

Scandinavia, which may be white to dark brown, is washed up on the east coast of Britain. Long extinct insects and leaves may be embedded in the amber. Carnelian, yellowish but deep orange in strong sunlight, is found in north-west Britain and on rocky slopes in North Wales.

The rocky coasts of Cornwall and Scotland may well yield blue and white aquamarine, and lovely green malachite, which gets its colour through contact with copper. In the Cairngorm mountains in Scotland, emeralds as well as blue-green topaz, green and gold beryl and stones used in Highland jewellery are found. The isles of Arran and Iona have long since produced

Polished stones can be used to model.

beautiful stones. Cat's eye jasper and rose quartz are Arran finds. The possibilities are endless to the observant, painstaking jewel-seeker.

Cutting, polishing and setting of stones may be done through a local jeweller; the fees are not usually excessive. However, if you intend making a lot of jewellery, you might consider buying a pebble tumbler for polishing your stones. The tumbler is basically a small barrel, rotated by an electric motor, inside which the stones tumble against one another, and are rounded and polished by an abrasive grit which must be added.

Once you have smooth, polished stones, the next step is to buy some metal mounts into which you can set them; you can buy mounts for making bracelets, earrings, cuff-links, rings and for pendants to hang on a chain. It is not necessary to drill holes in the stones in order to mount them, since there are now some adhesives available that have great strength and can safely be used to stick the stones on to the mounts.

Tumbled stones make attractive pendants.

Collecting seaweeds

The Victorians were ardent collectors of seaweeds, which they washed, dried and made into intricate and often striking wall decorations. As a schoolboy in the 'thirties, I spent much time in the summer holidays forking great mounds of the brown seaweed found on Anglesey beaches on to carts; this was transported to my grandparents' farm nearby, where it was spread over fields and then dug in as manure. Its use resulted in rich crops of broad beans, carrots and new potatoes the following year.

A beach is divided into zones: the splash zone at the top; the upper shore, covered only at high spring tides; the middle zone, which lies between the high and low water marks; and the low water zone, which is permanently covered. The upper shore and the upper reaches of the middle zone are the home of the green seaweeds. Three common types which you may find are the long, hollow strands of *Enteromorpha*, the attractive 'sea lettuce' and *Bryopsis*, a really beautiful seaweed with delicate fronds, found in sheltered spots.

The lower reaches of the middle zone is the area where the brown seaweeds thrive. There is an immense variety including the puzzling channel wrack – which dries out

A selection of the seaweeds that can be found on beaches.

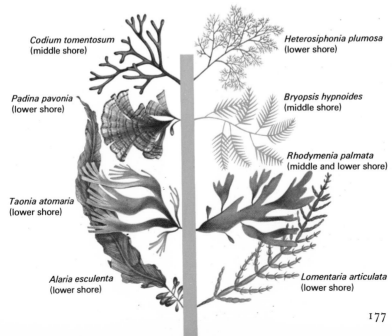

Codium tomentosum
(middle shore)

Heterosiphonia plumosa
(lower shore)

Padina pavonia
(lower shore)

Bryopsis hypnoides
(middle shore)

Rhodymenia palmata
(middle and lower shore)

Taonia atomaria
(lower shore)

Alaria esculenta
(lower shore)

Lomentaria articulata
(lower shore)

in brittle, black tufts on rocks at low tide but returns to its normal colouring when the tide returns – bladder wracks, huge saw-edged fronds, bootlace weeds and large oarweeds. A new brown seaweed found in Europe in recent years is a Japanese variety, which arrived as packing material around oysters!

The low water zone of the beach is the home of the red and pinkish-red seaweeds, whose form and beauty is remarkable. They may sometimes be found after storms cast high up the beach but will usually be seen in low water at low tide. Red seaweeds are sometimes difficult to identify, but this should not deter you from making a collection.

When you go collecting seaweeds it is a good idea to put them in polythene bags so that they stay moist and flexible. The illustrations show how to press the seaweeds so that they dry flat. Once dry, they can be used in all sorts of attractive ways. One idea is to arrange them on a piece of stiff paper, gluing them into position, and then you can have the arrangement framed to make an eye-catching picture. Or you could make shell and stone pictures and then decorate them with green and red seaweeds and small pieces of driftwood.

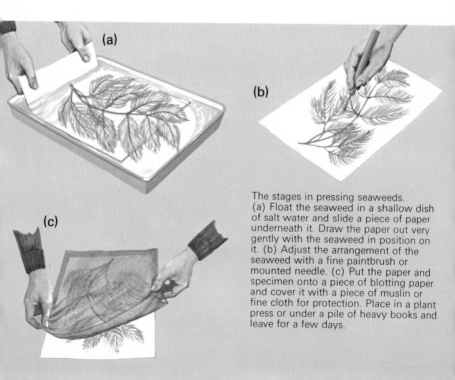

The stages in pressing seaweeds.
(a) Float the seaweed in a shallow dish of salt water and slide a piece of paper underneath it. Draw the paper out very gently with the seaweed in position on it. (b) Adjust the arrangement of the seaweed with a fine paintbrush or mounted needle. (c) Put the paper and specimen onto a piece of blotting paper and cover it with a piece of muslin or fine cloth for protection. Place in a plant press or under a pile of heavy books and leave for a few days.

Making a barbecue

Barbecues are good conservation practice for camping because timber is saved and the earth is left undisturbed. You can buy many excellent portable barbecues, which are lightweight, yet tough and hard-wearing. However, building a permanent barbecue for your own terrace or garden, your Scout or Guide headquarters, or the local sports club, is well worth the effort.

The barbecue shown on page 180 was designed originally for use in Kenya; it has since been made in many parts of the world with much success. Based on the standard size of British bricks (roughly 22·5 × 11 × 6·5 cm), it requires 400 bricks, but much money can be saved by building a brick frame, which uses 100 bricks, and filling the centre with rubble; the base can also be made of stones or rubble. Many of these barbecues have been made using second-hand bricks from demolition sites.

The grill bars can be ordered from a blacksmith, garage or iron-monger. The top grill is made of narrow iron bars for the food to cook on; the lower one is made of strips 2 cm wide and 75 cm long, set close together to hold the fuel. Altogether, for the top grill, you will need two bars 75 cm long to form the corners and two bars 65 cm long to form the side-bars on which all the other bars (55 cm long) will rest.

You will need the following tools to make your barbecue: one spade, two trowels, two buckets, a spirit level, a broomstick or string and stakes, and a plank. You will need good quality cement and some clean sand. Usually, it takes three people about two or three days to build. Choose the site carefully; it must be flat, firm ground that will not subside, and it must be in a sheltered position, but with the barbecue built so that the open side faces the prevailing wind for draught. Do not build the barbecue near any trees or scrub growth in case of fire.

Once you have chosen the site,

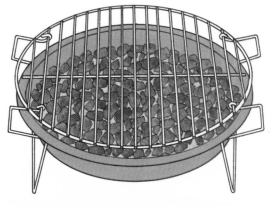

A portable, lightweight barbecue.

you should start by making the base. First, level the ground if necessary, then put down a layer of stones or rubble and cover with cement. When the cement has set hard you can measure out a square for the barbecue. Next, make the mortar; the recipe is six spades of sand to one of cement, mix, make a well in the middle, pour in water and mix to a wettish 'dough'.

Build up a square of bricks, five layers in all, as shown in the illustration, using the broom handle, or string and stakes, to get them absolutely straight. When the first row of bricks is bedded snugly, cover with mortar quickly. Wet each brick or stone used and work quickly, as dust and air loosen the structure.

Next, fill in the middle of the square with rubble, using mortar made with four spades of sand to one of cement; level off the top. You should then start laying bricks in the armchair pattern, shown in the illustration below.

When you have laid four complete courses of bricks, you should place the grill bars for the fuel across the barbecue, then build another layer of bricks to complete the barbecue. The food bars are kept loose and simply placed over the top brick course when you are going to use the barbecue.

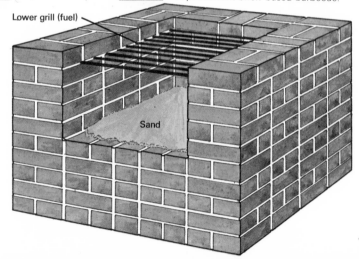

A permanent brick-based barbecue.

Making a hammock

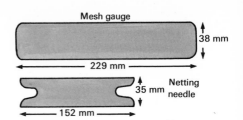

Mesh gauge

38 mm

229 mm

Netting needle

35 mm

152 mm

Hammocks are great fun to use in summer. You can camp under the trees without tents, with a light waterproof over your sleeping bag to offset dew. In winter they are used in Scout troop rooms when guests

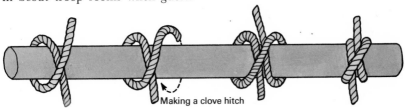

Making a clove hitch

are entertained. The hammock illustrated was designed for Sea Scouts afloat. The materials needed are: 22 metres of rope about 12 mm thick, two iron rings, and an ample supply of twine for meshing. The netting needle, gauge and battens are easily made from wood, but must be smoothed with sandpaper. The V-shape in the gauge carries the twine. Two knots only are used, the clove hitch and sheet bend, and one eye splice.

To make an eye splice untwist the strands of the rope for 23 cm to give three ends. Pass these ends through the iron ring; bend the rope back on itself to form the eye of the size required. See that the ends lie as stage (a) by tucking one end through a strand in the rope. Tuck the second end through the next strand (b). Now reverse the rope and tuck the third end through the third strand (c). All tucks are made against the lay of the rope. Repeat this cycle of

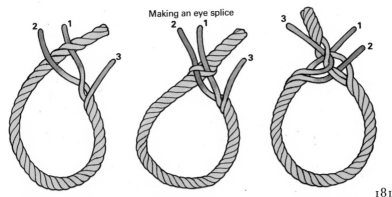

Making an eye splice

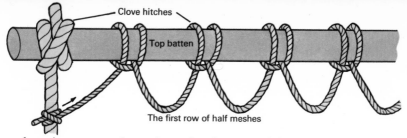

Clove hitches

Top batten

The first row of half meshes

tucks twice more and cut the ends short.

In net-making the operator always works from left to right, lashing the work up to a convenient beam, rafter or tree branch so that he can move freely round it from one side to the other.

How to make the framework

First of all you must make the framework for the hammock. Cut two four-metre lengths of rope. Secure one end of each piece of rope to an iron ring, using an eye splice, as described. Now take one piece of rope to either end of the first wood

batten and fix it with a clove hitch. Allow about 60 cm of rope between the ring and the ends of the batten.

Secure the second batten temporarily about 60 cm down from the top one. It is advisable to suspend a weight from the middle of this lower bar, as it will put tension on the side ropes and so help to keep the work uniform. As the mesh grows, this bar must move downwards until sufficient netting has been made. It is then finally secured and the stay-ropes are led from it to the second iron ring, to which they are attached with another eye splice.

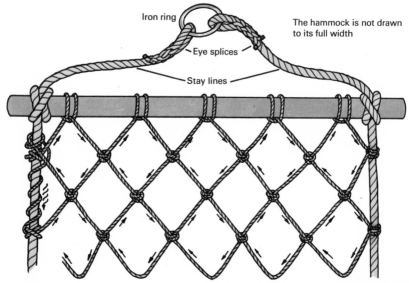

Iron ring

The hammock is not drawn to its full width

Eye splices

Stay lines

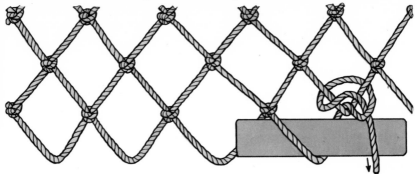

Net-making

First load the needle with twine. Then, with the framework secured to the rafter at a convenient working height, tie the end of the twine to the left-hand stay rope, just below the batten, with a clove hitch. Then make clove hitches along the batten at equal intervals until the right-hand end is reached, using the gauge to measure the half-mesh size.

To make the next row, move round to the other side of the framework, taking the twine round the stay rope and fastening it with a clove hitch. The mesh gauge is now used for the meshing proper. Hold it between the fingers and thumb of the left hand, and in line with the lowest hanging point of each of the half-meshes just made. The sheet bend is employed for the remainder of the work as shown above.

Lead the needle through the hanging half-mesh from back to front. Then take it to the right and form a loop; the needle must now lead the twine behind the mesh, round in front and down through the loop already made. Work the

knot taut. Notice that when the gauge is in place the twine is led from the previous knot in front of the gauge before it is taken to the rear to begin forming the sheet bend. Left-hand finger and thumb are used, still holding the gauge to position the knot.

On reaching the stay rope (left side in diagram opposite), fasten the twine to it with a half-hitch just above the last clove hitch and then wind the twine tightly down the stay in the lay of the rope to reach the starting point of the second row. Fasten with a clove hitch and continue net-making.

When the last row of mesh is reached, the work varies slightly in order to incorporate the second batten. Before each sheet bend is tied in the final row, take the twine to the batten and fasten there with a clove hitch. The drill, then, for the last row is: clove hitch to batten, sheet bend to mesh; clove hitch to batten, sheet bend to mesh, and so on.

Lastly, splice a third length of rope to each of the rings, for securing the hammock to its supports.

Making & flying kites

Kite flying has become extremely popular in recent years. A well-made kite will give hours of pleasure on the nearest common, park, beach, or field. However, you should always be very careful where you are flying your kite. *Make absolutely certain that it is not flown anywhere near electricity pylons carrying high-voltage power lines.* Unpleasant accidents can occur and even if there is no injury, considerable expense may be involved. Also, avoid all overhead telephone lines. Wide, open commons or wide, sandy beaches offer the best sites of all, and the right breezes.

It is interesting to recall that Franklin flew a kite in a thunderstorm to collect electricity, while the very first radio message ever sent across the Atlantic by Marconi used an aerial suspended from a kite in Cornwall. In the 19th century, kites were actually used to haul lightweight carriages along highways! In World War II, RAF airmen forced down into the sea hoisted radio aerials on kites from their rubber dinghies. The Germans actually had man-lifting kites with rotating wings like a helicopter. They were used to hoist men from submarines to spy out the horizon; the man aloft even had a telephone attached so that he could talk to his

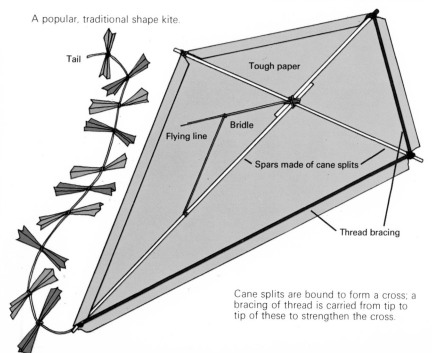

A popular, traditional shape kite.

Tail

Tough paper

Bridle

Flying line

Spars made of cane splits

Thread bracing

Cane splits are bound to form a cross; a bracing of thread is carried from tip to tip of these to strengthen the cross.

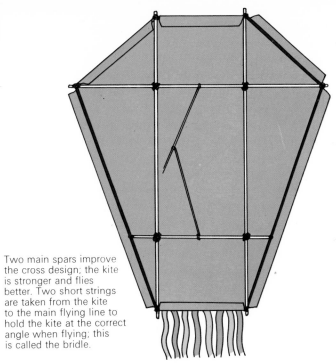

Two main spars improve the cross design; the kite is stronger and flies better. Two short strings are taken from the kite to the main flying line to hold the kite at the correct angle when flying; this is called the bridle.

submarine captain! Sometimes, in cases of immediate danger, the submarine dived to safety, cutting the observer loose on his kite as it did so.

Kites are best made with a tough paper sold at aeromodelling and games shops, often called bamboo paper; larger kites have been made successfully with tracing paper, several kinds of which are sold at stationers. The framework is made from bamboo canes, which may be bought in many sizes and thicknesses at garden centres and shops. They are called cane splits in some parts of the world. Spruce can also be used. The lighter bamboo canes

used for supporting tomatoes, small shrubs and flowers, are strong and efficient; they are usually about a metre in length. To split a cane, simply place a strong penknife blade in one end and give a sharp twist either way. The cane will split easily and can be smoothed with sandpaper. A proprietary brand of aeromodelling adhesive and strong thread for binding will complete the equipment. Thread bracing prevents any paper tearing.

The simplest form of kite uses cane splits in cross formation. Thread bracing stiffens and improves the cross, giving a good edge

The Hargreaves kite
One main spar and two cross-spars are
used; the cross-spars are braced at the
tips to form a semi-circular shape with
paper glued over the curve. Attach a
single line for flying at a point 8 cm
from the top of the main spar.

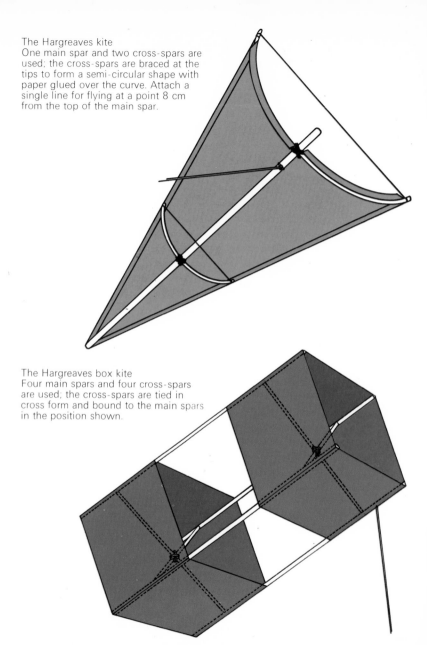

The Hargreaves box kite
Four main spars and four cross-spars
are used; the cross-spars are tied in
cross form and bound to the main spars
in the position shown.

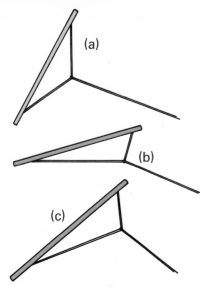

(a)

(b)

(c)

The trimming for flight: (a) the line is too low on the bridle and the kite will be unsteady; (b) too high, the kite will not rise at all; (c) this should give a good climb and steady flight.

for the paper to be fixed. The braced framework is placed on the paper and the shape marked out in pencil. Allowing a 1 cm overlap, cut out the paper with scissors; fold the overlaps upwards to make a shallow tray. Adhesive is now put lightly on the spars; the framework is placed in the tray and then, using

more adhesive, the overlap is stuck down over the thread bracing.

This system may be used for kites of varying design. One is illustrated on page 185, where two main spars have been used. This kite has extra resistance to wind; it is 60 cm high and 47·5 cm wide. Octagonal shapes make good kites; experiment with designs to suit the strength of prevailing breezes in the spaces available to you for kite flying. You may want to give your kite a tail, for although it is not essential, it does give some balance in the air. You should keep tails short. Use a paper streamer or a length of thread with wisps of paper knotted on it.

The Hargreaves kite is named after its Australian designer, an air pioneer; it is illustrated at the top of page 186. Hargreaves also designed the famous box kite, 30 cm square, regarded as the most efficient of all kites. To make this, two strips of paper are placed on a flat surface and the position of the spars is marked in pencil. Spars are then stuck on and the whole folded over so that the overlap is stuck to the opposite ends.

A selection of modern kites.

Cycling

Bicycles are more than a comparatively cheap means of getting around. The bicycle owner gets fresh air and exercise, has fun, avoids traffic jams and doesn't pollute the atmosphere. Sooner or later, all young people who enjoy the outdoor life will want to own a bike.

Recently, there have been variations on the conventional shape of a bike. Children from five years old up to teenagers can be seen on bikes with high-rise handlebars and long banana seats. These are fun bikes, for short journeys, and not recommended for outdoor adventurers. Small-wheeled bicycles with rubber suspension became very popular in the 1960s and can be good bikes for touring. Individual preferences will dictate the details of each person's bike, but a good basic model is shown in the illustration.

When choosing a bike, it is important to get the right size, and this is governed by the frame. As a rough guide, your inside leg measurement should be about 25 cm more than the length of the seat tube from where the pedals are hung to where the seat enters the frame. When sitting on the saddle you should just be able to reach the ground with both feet.

There are numerous parts to a bike, and the following notes will give you an idea of what to look for when buying and looking after your bike.

Saddles

Saddles can be adjusted for height and angle. The height should be enough for you to straddle the bike, as mentioned. Never raise the saddle so high that less than 5 cm of the pillar is within the frame.

Handlebars

If you intend to do a lot of cycling

Carrier

Spoke

Chain

you might prefer drop handlebars as they give a greater variety of hand positions. The top of the handlebars should be slightly lower than the top of the saddle.

Brakes

The commonest brakes are of the side-pull action, with the cable action at one side. Needless to say, good brakes are essential to the cyclist's safety. Check that the cables are tight and in good condition, that the blocks are not worn and that they connect properly with the wheel rim. Grease cables where they enter holes, and oil pivot points and brake levers. Make sure that you can operate brakes quickly.

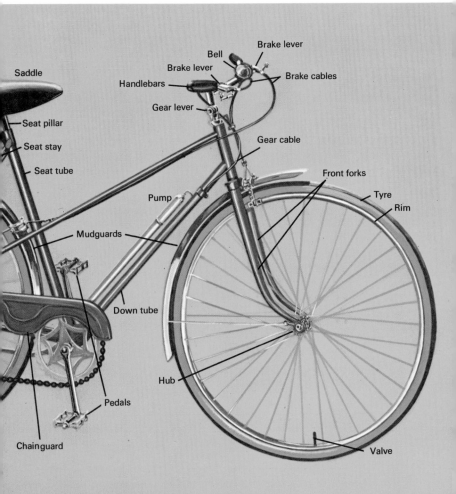

A modern 'fun' bike.

Gears

Gears enable the wheels to turn faster than you are pedalling. Derailleur gears are the commonest, although in Britain, Sturmey Archer gears are also popular. Make sure the gear lever is fastened tightly. Oil the gear cable at both ends.

Pedals

See that the pedals are screwed on tight.

Chain

Oil and clean the chain regularly, and make sure it is not loose.

Tyres

Check that tyres are not worn and that they are pumped up until they are as hard as you can make them.

In general, make sure that all nuts on your bicycle are tight, all moving parts well oiled, that frame and forks are not bent, that wheel spokes are not bent or missing and that the pump works. You will need a lamp for cycling at night and a red rear light.

It is a good idea to have your bike serviced once a year by a dealer, and you should always have your bike checked by a dealer after a knock. Where safety is concerned, such as in mending brakes or straightening forks, always go to a dealer to have the job done properly.

Once you have a bike, you will probably want to get out and see the countryside. A trip might last a day, or perhaps longer. So you will want to take a puncture kit, spanners, food, drink and other necessities. Have a rear carrier on your bike, and see that the nuts securing it are tight. Load your equipment evenly in panniers over the rear carrier.

Pay attention to your clothing. Make sure your shoes are comfortable. If you are uncertain of the weather, take extra sweaters in your pack. Woollen socks and jerseys are best in winter, and in summer a long sleeved shirt will prevent the sun making your arms sore. Don't wear flappy trousers that will get in the way of the pedals or chain, or if your trousers are wide-legged, use clips to prevent them flapping. Have a waterproof cape for wet weather.

Do not go far or venture into heavy traffic until you are absolutely confident about your cycling ability.

In Great Britain, the Royal Society for the Prevention of Accidents organises free cycling courses for children and awards proficiency badges and certificates. Get on such a course (they take place throughout Britain) and do not cycle on public roads until you have your badge.

The beautiful Swiss countryside offers good cycling to enthusiasts.

Your school, the police station, or your cycle shop will give you details of these courses.

Remember that all countries have laws governing the use of the roads, and that these apply to cyclists as well as motorists. So know the rules. In Britain, this means learning the Highway Code thoroughly.

Finally, common sense and consideration for others can help avoid accidents and worry. Do not ride 'no hands'. Do not give friends a lift on the cross-bar. Do not sneak a free ride by hanging on to a lorry. Save your family worry by telling them where you are going and when you expect to be back.

The study necessary to learn road-sense and to maintain your bicycle properly is time well spent. Cycling can be great fun. If you join a cycling club the fun can be shared and increased, and you could still be getting pleasure from cycling when your grandchildren are learning!

Cyclists stop to admire Tintern Abbey in Gwent, South Wales.

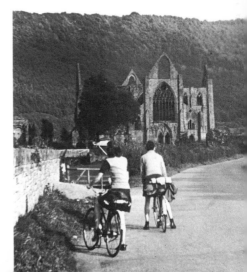

Conservation

Conservation in the widest sense means the wise and intelligent use by Man of all the natural resources in the world in which he lives. 'Man' means every boy and girl in the world just as much as adults. The supply of natural resources seems endless and is the basis of the high standard of living we enjoy today in many parts of the world. It *seems* endless, but is it? The answer must be 'No'. We must therefore be extremely careful how we use the resources available to us.

There are two main categories of resources. The first kind are the natural deposits of coal, in its many forms, natural gas, oil and minerals of all kinds, some of them far below the Earth's surface. Once these resources are used up they are gone for ever, so the first thing to learn about conservation is that we must not waste fuels like coal, gas and oil, or even electricity, which depends for its generation on other fuels.

Use compost heaps instead of bonfires.

Avoiding waste of any kind is a habit that every individual should acquire.

The second kind of natural resources concerns all outdoor enthusiasts. In includes soil, water, trees and other vegetation, and all wildlife. It also includes the air we breathe, since polluted air is one of the great evils of our time. Sound conservation practice must include a constant alert on the part of all human beings to see that we do not pollute the atmosphere that provides us with the means of life.

Garden bonfires cause air pollution.

Conservation and camping

It is very easy for campers to cause damage to living things, to the trees and plants and the wildlife that depends on them; if a camp site is used over and over again the turf is spoiled and may take a very long time to recover, if at all. The use of large wood fires, and fireplaces that have been dug out of the turf thoughtlessly, adds to the problem. Fire is a great killer of vegetation; forest and heath fires, often caused by carelessness, also destroy the homes and food of countless small wild creatures.

At one time, campers used to dig trenches round their tents to drain away rainwater if and when it came! Not only did this make the site look ugly, it also destroyed much valuable insect life and turf growth. Campers today should choose sites where rainwater drains away naturally and there is no risk of flooding. And, in the interests of conservation, you should cook economically using a primus stove or Camping Gaz in safe, protected places, which experience will teach you to select almost by instinct. However, if wood supplies are available in quantity through forestry thinnings, then small wood fires may sometimes be made using wood chips and small pieces of timber as required. Wood fire cooking is by hot, low embers not wasteful bonfires! Any wood fuel that is left over at the end of camp should be returned neatly for the use of other campers to come.

Heath fires, such as this one in Berkshire, destroy the homes of wild creatures.

There are many fires which help conservation practice. Charcoal fires in oil-drum halves and wood chip fires in tin-can stoves made from cooking oil containers or large tinned fruit cans or paint pots are just a few of the many. The illustrations on pages 98 and 99 show a selection of conservation fires, all of which have been used successfully.

The aim with all camping and camp cooking now should be to see that the site used is disturbed as little as possible and left exactly as Nature intended. Scouts and Guides have always practised conservation camping because their Founder, Robert Baden-Powell, said from the very beginning that when Scouts and Guides went camping they should leave nothing but their thanks when they returned home.

Living trees should never be cut down or damaged, and no one today should ever think of carving their initials on a tree trunk or of removing the bark from trees. Dead timber often exists on a mature, living tree such as an oak, and providing permission has been obtained from the owner of the site, or his agent or warden, it can be used for fuel supplies. In fact, the removal of dead branches from a tree is beneficial as it prevents them crashing to the ground in autumn and winter gales. The best way to trim off dead timber

Camping beneath Snowdon in Wales; always leave a campsite exactly as you find it.

Scouts use conservation fires for cooking.

is to use a Swedish bow saw; this most efficient tool, which uses a ribbon blade under tension, is an essential item of kit if wood fires are to be used in camp. It is lightweight, safe, efficient and easy to use. Keep the blade lightly oiled or use soap on it to prevent rust or damage; the blade should be protected with a length of old cycle tyre, tied in place with black tape. (Plastic is useless for this purpose; the protective sheath must be rubber.) It is quite safe for backpackers to carry a masked saw tied neatly on the side of their frame rucksack.

Do not be tempted to carry all the wet, rotting logs seen in the woods back to camp for the fire. Many of these old logs, which in fact are rotten branches that fell in gales, become the homes of all manner of tiny creatures. If the log is taken away, it looks neat and tidy but it destroys or damages the cycle that Nature has built up. Wet, rotting wood does not burn well anyway, but causes a lot of smoke; better to leave the old timber where it is in the long, damp grass or among the rotting leaves and concentrate on collecting new and recently fallen timber.

Know your country code

Learn how to look after trails in the woods, and on hillsides and river banks. Do not clear away leaves on woodland trails since they absorb rain; let Nature take its own course. Rotting leaves provide wonderful cover for small, wild animals and so, indirectly, are also important in providing food for wild birds in winter; watch how the blackbird searches long and diligently under hedges, in parks and on woodland floors, tossing leaves aside in the search for winter food.

Unthinking people on rambles and picnics frequently take short cuts between converging trails in the woods, or between public footpaths in the large wooded parks familiar

Never disturb woodland nature trails.

to all who live on the outskirts of cities, for example. If short cuts are taken regularly, then a whole area of trail is decimated; far better to plant some quick-growing shrubs to prevent short cuts, thus adding to the cover available for wildlife and improving the appearance. Local authorities are becoming conservation-minded. In my experience they welcome any constructive suggestions from anyone who regularly walks along country footpaths they control or areas of common and parkland.

'Low impact' walking is to be encouraged at all times when hiking. No short cuts should be taken across fields and certainly never across growing crops or hayfields. The only way for any conservationist to cross such fields is by the perimeter, walking as close to a hedge or wall as possible to avoid damage, opening and closing gates properly and making sure that if stone-step stiles have to be climbed over stone walls then no stones are dislodged, or if they are accidentally moved then they are replaced. Where a sheep has leapt over a stone wall, or a stone and turf wall, very common in North Wales for example, and knocked a stone or two, or a chunk of turf, out of place, then a good turn can be done to all concerned by repairing the damage on the spot. The stones are a good deal heavier than anyone may think, so be careful!

Wild flowers should never be picked and cast aside or taken home in bundles. Nature has her own methods of controlling the number of plants and animals. If, for example, bluebells get too thick on the ground then the resident badgers will see to it that they are thinned out; there is nothing badgers like more than bluebell bulbs, but they never seem to uproot and take them for food except when the bulbs need thinning out.

If you find a rare flower, leave it where it is: its position should be reported to some local expert, such as a botany teacher; if this is difficult, a

Some threatened European plants; from left to right: corn cockle, spring gentian, lady's slipper orchid, snake's head, fen orchid and cornflower.

telephone call or letter to the department of botany at the nearest university will result in the flower being traced. Know the local regulations concerning rare flowers as they vary from one country to another and a plant that is common in one country may be extremely rare and therefore protected by law in another. A very rare flower, the true ancestor of the carnation, was found by a boy hiking in the hills of North Wales; he had the good sense to pinpoint its position exactly on his map and report it to a university lecturer.

The common frog is one British animal in need of protection.

Mushrooms and toadstools, or fungi as they are more properly called, are often encountered on hikes and treks, growing both on the trunks of trees and on the ground. You will almost certainly have come across the field mushroom, which makes a tasty addition to bacon and eggs in the frying pan, but there are also many other fungi, both edible and poisonous, to be seen and located. In France, especially, the range of fungi is remarkable. Try to learn to recognize fungi with the aid of a book with coloured illustrations. Although some varieties are edible, you should never pick any yourself because they are difficult to identify and you could easily make the mistake of picking a poisonous one.

Conservationists in any country will know that there is many a fine meal to be had by taking advantage of Nature's larder, but they will always take care not to exploit it and risk upsetting the delicate balance that exists. In chapter two, I have shown how survival was no problem in mid-Norway, where we found delicious, grey, edible lichens growing everywhere on flat rocks in the unpolluted air, as well as freshwater shrimps in streams and all manner of sweet berries.

Protecting pond life

Far too many ponds are dirty and overgrown, particularly those in country areas, often in unsuspected places, neglected and known only to the wild ducks of winter months and the farmers whose sheep graze the area. Many plants and animals are now declining in numbers as a result of this deterioration in ponds. The decline of the common frog in Britain is one alarming example.

Frogs return to certain ponds to spawn; no one knows quite why

Cities also have conservation problems, as this dutch canal full of garbage shows.

Ponds get clogged up with a mass of decaying plant life in stagnant conditions and this destroys the creatures that live in the pond and normally keep the water fresh. The first move that is required to return a pond to its original healthy state is, obviously, to clear the pond of rubbish and litter, using tools such as garden rakes; the rubbish will need to be taken to some local dump. Old bikes, prams, decorator's refuse, unwanted fridges and gas stoves are some of the items that have been cleared out of ponds.

Once rubbish and vegetation debris have been raked out, the pond can breathe better. We have now taken the first step towards re-establishing the *ecosystem*, that is, a living community of plants and animals in which the organisms are dependent on one another, exchanging the materials of life and using them over and over. Life must go on; the cycle never ends.

In a pond, nutrients such as oxygen, calcium and phosphorus salts exist, some ready to be used immediately, others waiting in the sediment at the bottom. Then there is the pond's food factory, the tiny floating plants, or algae, which exist wherever the sunlight reaches. Larger floating plants and plants rooted in the bottom sediments will provide much-needed shelter and food for other living creatures.

The next stage in the pond cycle are the consumers. First the plant-eating animals, which live on the

certain ponds are used, but I can think of several on hiking trails, on golf courses and on commons. It seems likely that ponds in open situations, where the sun may well help in the hatching process, are more favoured. The female lays from one to two thousand eggs each year, but only a small proportion of these survive to become adult frogs.

Frogs are eaten by so many creatures: badgers, foxes, grass snakes, herons, to name only a few, but the greatest threat to their existence comes from school parties. The use of frogs may be very necessary in education but if the captured frogs could be allowed to form the nucleus of breeding units, perhaps using artificial ponds, then the sad case of the disappearing frogs could become a triumph for conservation.

Christleton Pit Conservation Project. Children from Christleton County Primary School in Chester carried out an ecological study of Christleton Pit, the site of an old marl pit, which won second prize in the 'Save the Village Pond Campaign'. Their work included the model shown top left. Because of the severe drought in 1975–6 it became necessary to change the study to practical pond rescue. Rubbish was removed, tons of silt and clay extracted and the surrounds re-shaped with the surplus material. New drains were dug to improve water supply, dykes were cut, and reed beds and other overgrown vegetation cleared to create habitats for plants and animals. The Parish Council helped with funds for mechanical diggers, while parents, friends and children provided the work force. The surrounds were grassed, new shrubs and trees planted and the water stocked with fish and other aquatic life. The project has been valuable not only for the detailed study, but also because it has shown that young people can become actively involved in the conservation of their environment.

green plants, then the meat-eaters, which feed on the plant-eaters. Finally, we have the decomposers, the bacteria and fungi that live in the pond but are mainly found in the silt and the muddy water at the bottom. They feed on dead animals, and their waste products, and dead plants. In turn they release more chemical substances, which are used in the never-ending cycle of life.

Study the pond closely. It may be natural or artificial. Does it have a stream inlet and outlet? Where does the water come from and go to? Watch for animals visiting the pond.

Early morning (4·30 am to 7 am) in spring and summer is the best time to watch wildlife in and around a pond. Take binoculars and a notebook, and find yourself a hide, a suitable bush in which you can sit or kneel on a folded groundsheet and watch for any activity.

Identify the plants and insects in and around the pond. Visit the local library and borrow a specialist book to show the types of plants that can be planted; water garden nurseries will sell them. I have planted bulrushes or similar rushes, many bog-loving plants, especially those with yellow globe flowers, Russian comfrey, foxgloves and, further from the edge of the pond, blackcurrants. I have also covered ugly stretches above the pond with Giant Himalayan blackberries, which take to this environment well and produce excellent cover for wild animals visiting the pond. Equipping the pond with snails, fish and other living creatures in the final task.

Watch the soil!

Campers and hikers should keep an eye on the ground and watch out

Swans drink from an ice-covered pond.

for soil erosion. Wherever surface water, resulting from heavy rain, has washed soil and plants away from gullies and steep hillsides there is the need to replenish it. It takes over a hundred years to make one inch of valuable topsoil. Imagine how many centuries of Nature's work is lost in one storm! To help prevent this, water can be diverted by digging suitable runoff channels, with the permission of the land owner if necessary.

Coastal sand can be kept in place by planting marram grass which has long, threadlike roots that help bind the sand particles together. The plants can initially be held in place with wire netting staked down or with hurdles. In situations where topsoil could be blown away by fierce winds, causing a minor dust-bowl, it can be kept in place, at least temporarily, with hurdles and tree branches if thinnings are available. Even groundsheets, well pegged down, have been used in windy situations.

Joining local projects

The best way to practise all-round conservation is to find out what is being done in your area and join in some scheme where your help will be valuable. Scouts and Guides will have their own plans and there is always much to be done on the many large camping grounds which the two associations own and run. Otherwise, the Junior Conservation

Scouts help in a conservation project.

Corps, the Wildlife Youth Service, the Junior Bird Recorders of the Royal Society for the Protection of Birds and many other societies will welcome help in their schemes.

Wherever it is possible, keep planting shrubs to provide cover for wildlife, keep providing wildlife with food, especially in winter, and water in suitable frost-free containers, and offer help whenever it can usefully be employed in conservation. You cannot do more than that and generations to come will grow up in a world that will benefit.

Scouts collect paper for re-cycling.

Nature Spotting

Wherever you are outdoors, you can almost always be sure to come across some plant or animal. Even in the centre of cities, birds and other animals have learned to live with man; moss grows among the paving stones, and trees, which are the homes of small creatures such as insects, line many streets. Many cities have parks, of course, and here a surprisingly large variety of wild-life can be found. And why shouldn't this be so? After all, many parks create almost the exact conditions that birds, foxes, rabbits and insects find in the wild.

Looking at plants and animals is great fun, and it is quite easy to see many interesting sights on a country walk, in a park, or even in your garden if you have one. Many trees and flowers are easy to spot, because they are big, or brightly coloured. To see some of the smaller flowers, mushrooms or mosses, however, you may have to search, sometimes on your hands and knees, peering between blades of grass.

Think of each place you visit, such as a pond or a wood, as a living community – rather like a town.

Likewise with animals, several types of birds and insects are easy to see, but to see a shy fox or rabbit, you will usually have to sit quietly and wait for them to pass near you, or creep near them very slowly and stealthily. To do this, it is often useful to locate the animals' burrows. You will probably find that droppings are a good indication of the whereabouts of a particular animal, as they are often found near the entrances to burrows.

Some other useful signs to look for are animal tracks. These can usually be found in mud, and although they may often belong to dogs or other domestic animals, those of foxes and badgers and a variety of birds may be seen. Feathers, too, are an indication of which birds may be found in the area. When preening, birds often pull out and drop old or damaged feathers, which fall from the tree or other site they are perched on at the time.

Trees are the home of a surprising variety of animals, and a tree such as an oak will often reveal many interesting small creatures living among the safety of its leaves and branches if you look closely. Bigger animals like squirrels and birds may also be hiding among the branches.

In other words, to obtain the most from studying nature outdoors, search carefully and thoughtfully. A rotting log, a pile of leaves, or a clump of grass are all worth a close look, for these are the types of places

Key

Throughout the following pages on nature spotting, numbers and letters will be used to indicate the best places, and the best times of the year, to find many of the plants and animals described. Do not be surprised, however, if some plants and animals sometimes turn up in different places to those indicated.

1 = Spring
2 = Summer
3 = Autumn
4 = Winter
A = Woodland
B = Meadow
C = Hedgerow
D = Heathland
E = Moorland
F = Pond
G = River
H = Rocky shore
J = Sandy shore
K = Roadside

Bold type denotes the places, or the times of the year, when particular wildlife is most common or at its best for studying.

where interesting finds are made.

It is worth joining your local naturalists' society if there is one. They always welcome and encourage new members, and from them you may gain some useful information about interesting places to visit. Plan your trips wisely. Decide exactly where you are going to go, and take with you any equipment you may need. If possible, visit each place as often as you can. A particular spot may yield nothing of interest one day, but may surprise you with the abundance of its wildlife the next. Weather conditions and the time of year can make a lot of difference.

Finally, wherever you are, practise conservation. Do not pick flowers or destroy wild plants, and collect animals only for examination and then release them unharmed. Not only will this ensure that our wildlife heritage is maintained, and that there will be plenty for others to see, but it will prove that you are a good naturalist.

On the following pages, we shall look at a few examples from the main groups of animals and plants that you are likely to come across. We shall see where they are most likely to be found and something of their ways of life.

A selection of the equipment you may need for nature spotting: sweep net with a long pocket which can be swept through grass or hedges to catch insects; fishing or shrimp net for finding small pond animals and using in rock pools on the seashore; magnifying glass; hand trowel which can be used in finding the small animals that live just below the surface of soil or sand; plastic specimen tubes which are useful containers for examining specimens. You should always keep a notebook and pencil to hand for recording your observations.

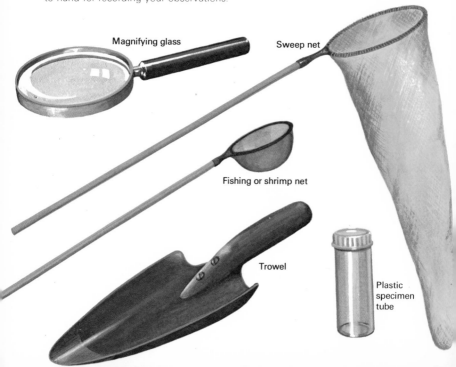

Magnifying glass

Sweep net

Fishing or shrimp net

Trowel

Plastic
specimen
tube

A selection of fungi.

Fungi

Key = 1 2 **3 A** (especially on rotting tree stumps, and among the grass growing under trees) **B** C D E K.

For most of the year, fungi exist underground, or in rotting logs and other damp places, as a series of tiny threads called a *mycelium*. At certain times of the year, however, usually in late summer and autumn, especially after rain, the mycelium sprouts a *fruiting body*. On this fruiting body are borne the spores that will disperse to give rise to new fungal colonies. The familiar mushrooms and toadstools shown above are the fruiting bodies of some fungi. Other fungi have fruiting bodies that resemble trumpets, or clubs. Those on the right of the picture below resemble bird's nests, and indeed are called bird's nest fungi.

Some spores are carried away by wind as they drop from fruiting bodies. Others are dispersed when a splash of rain lands on the edge of the fruiting body, forcing the light, dusty spores out through the top.

Fungi do not make their own food as green plants do, but obtain nourishment by absorbing the 'juices' from other plants, both dead and living (and sometimes from animals, too). Some fungi are poisonous, so never eat any, except those that you buy from shops for that purpose, and always wash your hands after handling wild fungi.

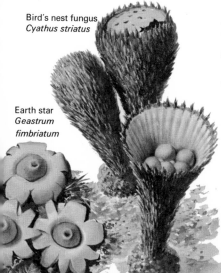

Bird's nest fungus
Cyathus striatus

Earth star
Geastrum fimbriatum

Seaweeds

Key = 1 2 3 4 **H** (sheltered rocky shores are best, because here the gentler seas allow the young seaweeds to attach themselves to the rocks in greater numbers) J (a few seaweeds are found on rocky outcrops, or washed up by the sea).

Walk along the seashore and sooner or later you will come across seaweeds. There may be a few odd strands washed up after rough weather or great bands, sometimes covering huge areas of rock, and stretching way below the low tide mark. Look more closely and you will see that there are red, green and brown seaweeds. Although all seaweeds contain the green pigment *chlorophyll*, some also contain red or brown pigments and these mask the green colour of chlorophyll.

Seaweeds are primitive plants, but they are well equipped to survive in the sea. Notice how firmly they are attached to the rocks by their holdfasts, and feel the slippery, rubbery texture of their bodies (or *thallus*), which offers little resistance

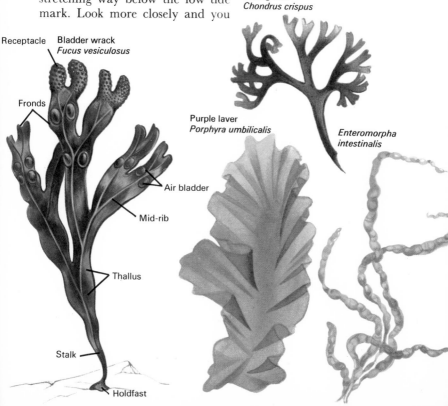

Carragheen
Chondrus crispus

Receptacle   Bladder wrack
Fucus vesiculosus

Fronds

Purple laver
Porphyra umbilicalis

Enteromorpha intestinalis

Air bladder

Mid-rib

Thallus

Stalk

Holdfast

to the water and so allows them to sway with the waves. One of the most interesting features of seaweeds is the way in which each type is suited to live in a different position on the shore. Those types that cannot stand too much submersion live high up the beach, and those that need plenty of water are found near the low tide mark. This arrangement is called *zonation*.

Mosses

Key = 1 2 3 **A** (especially on trees), D (on rocks) F G (in damp places near the water) **K** (on the tops of walls).

Because of their small size (usually only a few millimetres in height) mosses are often overlooked, but these interesting plants are well worth studying, especially with the aid of a magnifying glass. To the casual observer most mosses look the same, but look more closely and you will find a great variety of leaf shapes and arrangement. Mosses are made up of two distinct parts: the green leafy plant that can be found all the year round; and the tiny capsules born on long stalks, which are the reproductive structures and are produced only in late summer. The capsule and its stalk are usually coloured green to begin with, but then turn brown like those in the picture.

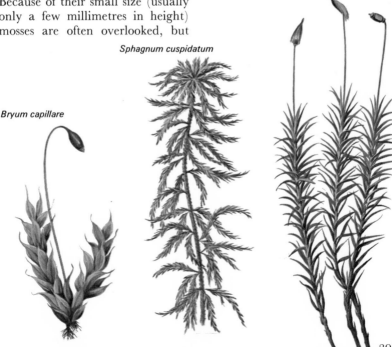

Polytrichum commune

Sphagnum cuspidatum

Bryum capillare

Royal fern
Osmunda regalis

Ferns

Key = 2 3 A C **D** E K.

Ferns are more complex plants than mosses. From a root-like structure called a *rhizome*, they produce leaves, or *fronds*, which in some types may grow to a metre in length. If you look at the underside of many fronds in late summer you will see small brown patches on them. These are the reproductive structures called *spores*. However, some ferns, such as the royal fern shown here, bear spores on a spike.

Hart's tongue fern
Phyllitis scolopendrium

Bracken
Pteridium aquilinum

Larch cone

Juniper sprig with fleshy, berry-like cones

Pine sprig with needle-shaped leaves and cone

Blue spruce *(Picea pungens)*

Two varieties of larch *(Larix decidua)*

Cone of blue spruce

Conifers

Key = 1 2 3 4 **A** D.

Conifers are found mainly in cooler parts of the world, where they often form large forests. There are many types of conifer, but they all share certain features. Firstly, they have needle-shaped leaves which are shed all the year round, but are being replaced continuously so that the trees are never without leaves. Secondly, they produce seeds borne in cones. In dry, windy weather the cones open and the seeds are scattered. In some areas, such as hilly, sandy places, conifers and broad-leaved trees grow together. Birch and pine are often found growing together in this way; woods where this occurs are called mixed woods.

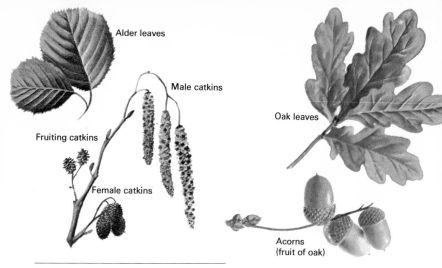

Alder leaves

Male catkins

Oak leaves

Fruiting catkins

Female catkins

Acorns
(fruit of oak)

Broad-leaved trees

Key = 1 2 3 **A** B D F G.

To many people, walking through a woodland of broad-leaved trees is one of the most enjoyable ways to study nature outdoors. Where else can one find such an array of interesting plants and animals?

Broad-leaved trees belong to the large group of plants known as *angiosperms*, which also includes the flowering plants and shrubs. Unlike conifers, most broad-leaved trees are

Common alder
Alnus glutinosa

Common oak
Quercus robur

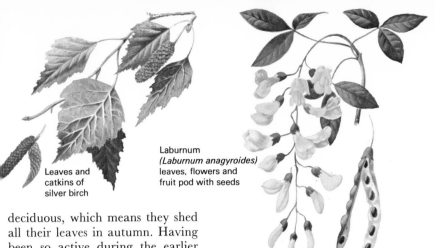

Leaves and
catkins of
silver birch

Laburnum
(Laburnum anagyroides)
leaves, flowers and
fruit pod with seeds

deciduous, which means they shed all their leaves in autumn. Having been so active during the earlier part of the year producing fruit, they slow down and rest in winter in preparation for the following spring. Like all angiosperms, broad-leaved trees produce flowers, but although in a few types (such as the cherry tree, horse chestnut and laburnum) they are big and bright, the flowers of most trees are small and dull in colour. Spring is the best time of the year to see trees in flower.

The fruit of trees is usually much easier to see than the flowers; apples, beechnuts, acorns and chestnuts are fruits which you will often find. In summer, one of the best ways to tell trees apart is to study their leaves, using a good book which shows what each looks like.

Silver birch
Betula pendula

Horse chestnut
(Aesculus hippocastanum)
in flower with
detail of fruit

Flowers

Key = 1 **2** 3 A B C D E F G K.

Flowers can be found in nearly every kind of habitat, as the key shows. Although flowers are so widespread, they are sometimes only locally common, or grow in small groups. However, you should have no trouble in spotting quite a few of the more common wild flowers, such as the ones illustrated on these pages. Even those that are sometimes pests and are therefore known as 'weeds' are quite often very beautiful.

Just as mushrooms and toadstools are only part of a particular plant (the part that helps to create the next generation), the same is true of flowers. Flowers are the part of the plant concerned with reproduction. Many flowering plants need insects to help them in their reproductive processes. The insects transfer pollen from one flower to another while visiting the flower to drink the nectar it produces.

Many flowers are pollinated by a wide variety of insects such as flies, beetles and bees; these flowers are usually large and brightly coloured, and have a very open arrangement of petals to allow the insects 'easy entry'. Other flowers are more particular about which insects visit them. This is one way of ensuring that the insect will visit another flower of the same type, which is very important because flowers can only be pollinated by pollen from other flowers of the same type. Such flowers usually have their petals in

Field poppy
Papaver rhoeas

Red clover
Trifolium fragiferum

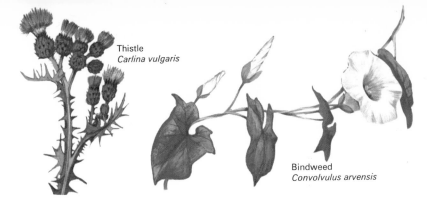

Thistle
Carlina vulgaris

Bindweed
Convolvulus arvensis

the form of a long tube, so that only long-tongued insects, such as butterflies, visit to reach the nectar at the flower's base. Try studying a few different types of flowers and make a list of the kinds of insect that visit each of them.

You will certainly come across a great variety of flowers when you are out walking, but only a very few can be included here. What you will soon notice for yourself is that some types of flowering plants grow best in certain areas. For example, sandy heathland is particularly favoured by gorse and heather. Heather is also found in large quantities on the higher moorland. Flowers such as iris and rushes prefer to grow near the edge of water. Actually growing in the water are the specialized aquatic plants, such as water lilies, crowfoot and duckweed. Fields of poppies are a common sight during early summer. A few flowering plants prefer the stiff winds of the seashore, and cliffs are a good place to find flowers such as the sea aster.

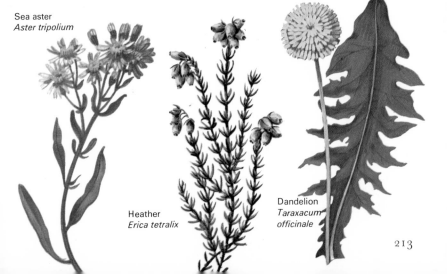

Sea aster
Aster tripolium

Heather
Erica tetralix

Dandelion
Taraxacum officinale

213

Slugs, snails and shellfish

Key = 1 2 3 4 B C F **H** (especially hiding among rock crevices, clinging to the rocks or to seaweeds growing on the rocks) **J** (usually buried in the sand).

The correct scientific name for the group of animals that includes snails, slugs, clams, oysters and, in fact, most of what we often call 'shellfish', is the *molluscs*. Squids and octopuses are also molluscs, but they, like the slug, have done away with their protective outer shell. Snails can often be found in meadows and hedgerows, and also in ponds, but one of the most exciting places to look for them is on the seashore. Molluscs like the periwinkle, whelk and topshell are usually found on rocky shores. They creep about among the rocks and seaweed with their broad, flat foot, and can retreat into their shell if danger threatens. The scallop and razor shell have hinged shells, and each has a powerful spade-like foot with which it can dig very rapidly into the sand.

Common periwinkle
Littorina littorea

Common cockle
Cerastoderma edule

Garden slug
Arion ater

Common whelk
Buccinum undatum

Great scallop
Pecten maximus

Razor shell
Ensis siliqua

Crabs, lobsters and shrimps

Key = 1 2 3 4 F **H** J.

Pictured here are some more animals you may see if you visit a rocky seashore. These animals all belong to the group known as the *crustaceans*. The shrimp, which is often found in rock pools, has a relative, the freshwater shrimp, which might well appear in your net when you are pond-dipping. Small crabs can be found among the seaweeds growing on rocks, but more often under rocks on the lower shore.

Although crabs and their relatives have hard coverings to their bodies like molluscs, it is incorrect to think of these as shells, because this hard body covering is really the animal's skeleton. It is called the *exoskeleton* (or outside skeleton), and is like a suit of armour, enclosing the soft body. Insects also have their body parts protected by an exoskeleton. Also, unlike molluscs, crabs and other crustaceans have jointed legs with which they can scuttle along quite quickly in search of food. The powerful pincers that many crustaceans possess are really one of their pairs of legs. Nature has turned them into weapons for dealing with prey or defending themselves.

Crabs and lobsters feed by eating other living animals and also by scavenging for the dead remains of animals. The hermit crab has a soft body, and uses the old shells of molluscs for a protective home.

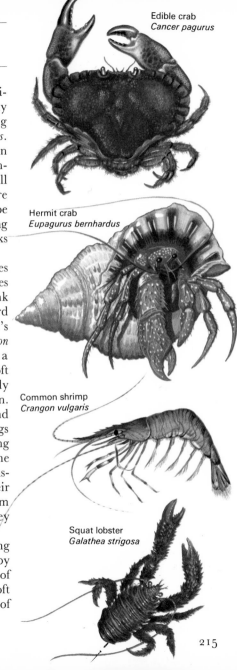

Edible crab
Cancer pagurus

Hermit crab
Eupagurus bernhardus

Common shrimp
Crangon vulgaris

Squat lobster
Galathea strigosa

215

Insects

Key = **1 2 3** 4 A B C D E F G H J K.
Of all animals, insects are by far the most numerous and diverse. In fact, there are more different types of insect than there are every other type of animal put together! Although we commonly see bees, flies, ants, and beetles such as ladybirds there are, hidden in the soil and under the bark of trees, vast numbers of insects which we seldom see.

Many people get confused and think that spiders are insects, but if you remember the following points it should be easy to tell an insect from any other creature.

1 All adult insects have a body divided into three parts: head, thorax and abdomen. Spiders have two main divisions to their bodies.

2 All adult insects have three pairs of legs, and these are all found on the middle part of the body, the thorax. Spiders have four pairs of legs, all on the first part of the body.

3 Most insects have one or two pairs of wings (no other animals apart from birds and bats have true wings) and these are found on the thorax too. Sometimes one pair of wings acts as a protective case, hiding the second pair from view when the insect is not flying. This is so in beetles.

As you can see from the key, insects can be found almost anywhere, and at almost all times of the year, although many are at their most numerous in spring and summer. Examine the bark and leaves of trees carefully, and you will find beetles, larvae (the young stage of insects), moths and weevils. Crickets and grasshoppers abound in the meadow grass, and wherever flowers grow there will be bees, butterflies and other insects visiting to drink the nectar. Woods are one of the favourite habitats of the industrious

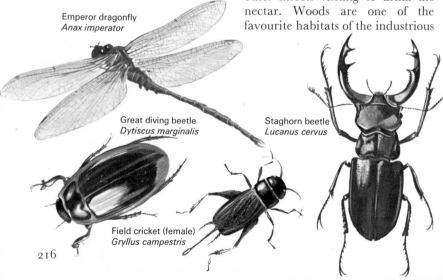

Emperor dragonfly
Anax imperator

Great diving beetle
Dytiscus marginalis

Staghorn beetle
Lucanus cervus

Field cricket (female)
Gryllus campestris

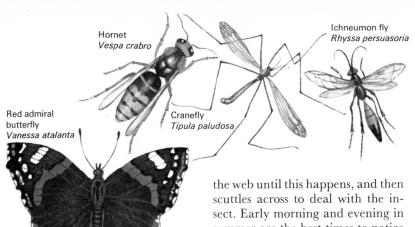

Hornet
Vespa crabro

Ichneumon fly
Rhyssa persuasoria

Cranefly
Tipula paludosa

Red admiral
butterfly
Vanessa atalanta

ant, although you can often find ants' nests under stones in your garden or local park. Ponds and rivers have a special interest for many entomologists (people who study insects), for here are found dragon-flies and their fearsome larvae; water boatmen, which skim across the water surface; the great diving beetles and interesting larvae like those of the caddis fly, which build a protective 'coat' of shells and stones around themselves.

Spiders

Key = 1 **2** 3 4 A B C D F K.
Spiders are usually less noticeable than insects, although they are just as fascinating to watch as they go about their daily lives. Many spiders spin sticky, silky webs in which small flying insects become trapped. The spider usually hides at the edge of the web until this happens, and then scuttles across to deal with the insect. Early morning and evening in summer are the best times to notice spiders' webs outdoors, but old buildings also often provide places for spiders to spin their webs. Instead of making webs, some spiders lie in wait for suitable prey to pass by, and then quickly pounce and overcome it. A few kinds of spiders actively hunt for small animals to eat.

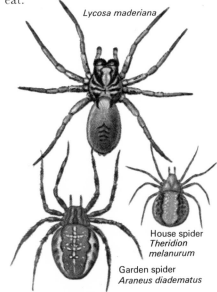

Lycosa maderiana

House spider
Theridion melanurum

Garden spider
Araneus diadematus

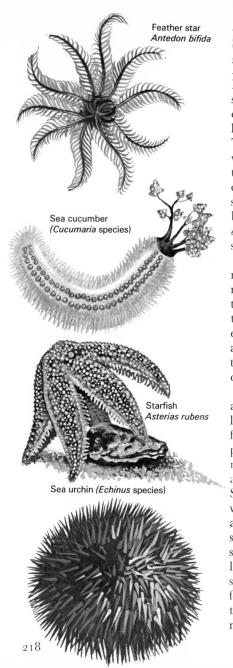

Feather star
Antedon bifida

Sea cucumber
(Cucumaria species)

Starfish
Asterias rubens

Sea urchin *(Echinus* species)

Starfishes, sea urchins and sea cucumbers

Key = 1 2 3 4 H (especially under stones and in rock pools) J (especially lying just under the sand near low water).

The seashore is the only habitat where you will find starfishes and their relatives the sea urchins, sea cucumbers, brittle stars and feather stars. All these different creatures belong to the group of animals called *echinoderms* (animals with spiny skins).

All adult echinoderms have remarkable bodies based on a five-rayed pattern. In most starfishes this is clearly seen, but in some other types of echinoderm it is much less easy to spot. Although echinoderms appear to be strange, lowly creatures, they are in fact one of man's closest ancestors!

Echinoderms are most numerous around rock pools or stones near the lower shore. Starfishes can often be found among mussel beds for, as the picture here shows, they prise open mussel shells with their powerful arms in order to eat the mussels. Some echinoderms have long stalks which attach them to the seabed, and they wave their arms about in search of food. All the echinoderms shown here, however, are free-living, and actively roam about searching for food. The starfish and feather star move about by using their 'arms', and the sea urchin by means of its spines.

Blenny *(Blennius* species)

Eel
Anguilla anguilla

Fishes

Key = 1 2 3 4 F G H.

The fishes shown on this page are just a very few of the many different types that live in rivers, lakes or the sea. Fishes are a little more difficult to spot than most other animals because it is not usually possible to see very clearly in water, and because fishes blend in well with their background when seen from above. However, if you keep still and look into a shallow river, say from a bridge, you can often see fishes lying facing the current as they wait for food to be carried to them. A piece of bread tossed on to the surface of a river or lake will also attract fishes.

The stickleback is a common, fierce little fish found in ponds, and is easy to catch with a small net. The minnow, too, is a small fish of ponds and rivers and is easily caught. The eel is a long, thin fish which lives in lakes and rivers but migrates to the sea to spawn. After spawning, the tiny, new-born eels somehow find their way back to the rivers and lakes that their parents journeyed from. Eventually they, too, have the urge to spawn and make the journey back to the sea. Eels are sometimes found wriggling across land from one stretch of water to another.

Rock pools are a good place to spot sea fishes, because small specimens like the blenny often become trapped in them as the tide goes out. Again, you will normally have to sit quietly for a few minutes and wait for the fish to come out from its hiding place under a piece of seaweed or a stone. The weever is an unpleasant customer that lies partly buried in shallow water. It has a row of poisonous spines on its back.

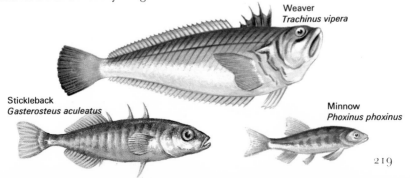

Weever
Trachinus vipera

Stickleback
Gasterosteus aculeatus

Minnow
Phoxinus phoxinus

219

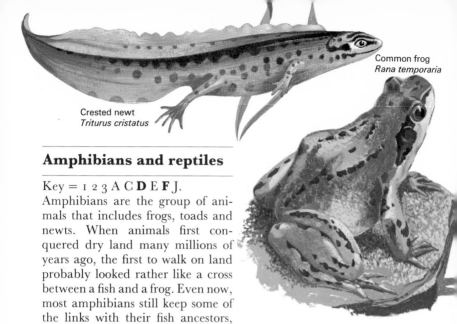

Crested newt
Triturus cristatus

Common frog
Rana temporaria

Amphibians and reptiles

Key = 1 2 3 A C **D** E **F** J.

Amphibians are the group of animals that includes frogs, toads and newts. When animals first conquered dry land many millions of years ago, the first to walk on land probably looked rather like a cross between a fish and a frog. Even now, most amphibians still keep some of the links with their fish ancestors, for they must return to water to lay eggs and begin life.

In spring, the familiar frog's spawn (really the eggs, looking like a mass of jelly with dark specks) can be seen near the edges of ponds. From this hatch tiny tadpoles, which soon develop into froglets and, eventually, frogs. During the summer months the frogs live near the water, catching insects and grubs, and when winter comes they hide in holes until spring.

Reptiles are animals such as lizards and snakes. They have scaly skins and teeth, unlike amphibians, and feed on a great variety of small creatures. Reptiles prefer warm weather because their body temperature is almost the same as that of their surroundings. Among the best places to find lizards and snakes are heaths, where they often sun themselves on rocks, and by old stone walls near woods and hedgerows.

Common lizard
Lacerta vivipara

Birds

Key = **1 2** 3 4 **A B** C **D E F G H** J K.
Of all living creatures, birds must be among the most exciting to watch. Many types are very easy to spot, and many of the less well-known birds can still be seen and studied if you are quiet, patient, and go about it in the correct way. Although not essential, two items of equipment greatly increase the fun to be had from bird watching. One is a pair of binoculars. Binoculars will open up a new world for the naturalist and are a very worthwhile item for which to save. For the beginner, a pair that have '8 × 30' stamped on them are best, since they are powerful enough to use for most bird watching, but will also be useful for watching other forms of wildlife.

The second very important item is a field guide to birds. In fact, a field guide to all the groups of animals and plants we have looked at so far is useful, but since birds can fly away so quickly when alarmed, and because there are so many different types, it is useful to try and identify them as soon as you have spotted them. Try also to keep a notebook with up-to-date observations such as the types of bird you see on, say, a lake, or in a wood, and note any changes that occur throughout the year.

On the following pages we shall have a brief look at the best places and times of the year to spot birds and discover what they are doing.

Woods

This is one of the favourite haunts of many types of birds – woodpeckers, jays, thrushes, blackbirds, magpies and crossbills are just a few of the many types you should be able to spot. In spring, you should see the

Magpie
Pica pica

Jay
Garrulus glandarius

Swallow
Hirundo rustica

males flying from tree to tree, singing in each one to proclaim their territory and attract a mate. Nest building is another sight worth watching for. You may not actually see the well-hidden nest, but you will very likely spot the birds constantly flying back to, and disappearing among the branches of the same tree with twigs and other nest material in their beaks.

Meadows

In summer, you will find birds such as pipits and larks visiting the meadows looking for insects and other food to eat. In winter many fields and meadows are visited by lapwings and gulls, which usually collect in flocks.

Hedgerows

The seeds and berries of hedgerows provide food for many small birds, and flocks of tits and finches are common here, as well as wrens and sparrows. Some birds use hedgerows for nesting.

Heathland and Moorland

These areas often have little cover to offer birds except for gorse bushes and small trees, and here we find the shrike, a handsome bird which catches insects, lizards and other animals and impales them on its 'larder' of thorns or wire. Curlews,

Pheasant (cock)
Phasianus colchicus

Wren
Troglodytes troglodytes

Blackbird
Turdus merula

wheatears and grouse are common. Wheeling aloft you may well spot predatory birds such as the buzzard, merlin or kestrel.

Ponds and Rivers

Many waterbirds are to be found here, including ducks, coots, moorhens, swans and grebes. The king-fisher is a common, but beautiful, small bird that lives by water and 'fishes' by diving into the water to catch its prey in its long beak.

Seashores

The cries of gulls and the 'kleep' of oystercatchers are familiar sounds on many coasts, and these and other seabirds such as cormorants and plovers are easy to see. Gulls are scavengers and they will happily eat fishes, food left by humans and many other things. It is interesting to see how different birds have developed to live and feed in different ways. Thus oystercatchers have long bills for probing into the mud and sand; turnstones and plovers have short

Herring gull
Larus argentatus

bills for searching among seaweeds; and gulls and cormorants have sharper, heavier bills for dealing with fishes.

Reservoirs and gravel pits

These man-made structures have become some of the most important areas to see many interesting birds such as gulls, herons, cormorants, lapwings, ducks and waders.

Roadsides

Throughout the year, you will see sparrows, crows, rooks, starlings and kestrels here. The vibrations of the traffic help bring worms and other small animals to the surface for the birds to feed on.

House sparrow
Passer domesticus

Moorhen
Gallinula chloropus

Starling
Sturnus vulgaris

Mammals

Key = 1 2 3 4 A B C D E G.

Many mammals are only active at night, and even those that can be seen by day are shy, so they must be approached with extreme caution, or they will have vanished before you even set eyes on them. One of the most common mammals is the squirrel. There are two main kinds of squirrel, the red squirrel, which lives mostly in pine forests, and the grey squirrel, which is often found in broad-leaved woods. For most of the year, squirrels are active creatures, running along the ground or jumping from tree to tree in their search for food. The squirrel's nest, or drey, is built high up in the branches of a favourite tree.

Although mostly active by night, the fox can also be seen by day, usually hunting near the edges of woods and hedgerows, or running across fields. Foxes feed mainly on

A red deer.

worms, insects, small mammals and birds but they sometimes go into towns in search of food.

Rabbits live in groups in underground burrows called warrens. They are most easily seen in the early morning and at dusk when they emerge from their burrows to find food. Many people get rabbits and hares mixed up, but all you need to remember is that hares are reddish in colour with long, black-tipped ears and rabbits are grey with much shorter ears.

Deer are very shy creatures of woodlands and moors. One of the best places to study them is in large parks, where herds are often kept. The badger and otter are seldom seen, mainly because they are nocturnal (active only at night). One of the best ways to see if these or other mammals are about is to look for their footprints or droppings.

Hare
Lepus capensis

Rabbit
Oryctolagus cuniculus

grey squirrel
(*Sciurus carolinensis*)

fox
(*Vulpes vulpes*)

badger
(*Meles meles*)

otter
(*Lutra lutra*)

trout
(*Salmo trutta fario*)

A Guide to the Earth

It used to be thought that our planet, the Earth, was born as a flaming, hot ball. It is still not certain how it was formed but many scientists believe that the Earth began about 4500 million years ago from the cold accumulation of dust and gases that surrounded the Sun at that time.

We live upon the outside 'skin' of the Earth, called the *crust*, together with other animals and plants on which we depend. We are beginning to understand more about the make-up and workings of the interior of our planet with the help of the often catastrophic earthquakes.

When an earthquake occurs, it sends out a series of shock waves of different types, which pass through the Earth in different times, or sometimes not at all, depending upon the nature of the material. By looking at the arrival records of these shock waves, called *seismograms*, at points around the world, scientists called *geologists* and *seismologists* have been able to build up quite a detailed model of the structure and composition of the inside of the Earth.

The Earth seems to consist of layers of different materials rather in the same way that an onion is made up. In the very centre of the Earth is the *core*, which itself is probably made up of two layers. The inner core is thought to be made of metals such as iron and nickel, but at this depth, a given volume of the core may be as much as seventeen

Earthquake waves travelling through the planet.

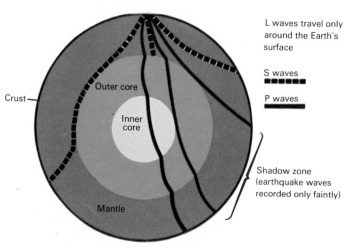

L waves travel only around the Earth's surface

S waves

P waves

Crust

Outer core

Inner core

Mantle

Shadow zone (earthquake waves recorded only faintly)

CRUST

Ocean 6 km

MANTLE

2900 km

CORE

Liquid 2000 km

Solid 1370 km

A look into the centre of the Earth: the planet is composed of a two-layered central core surrounded by a mantle, which is in turn enveloped by the crust on which we live. Knowledge of the Earth's interior has come from earthquake study.

times heavier than the same volume of water. The outer core is also iron and nickel but in a hot liquid form. Around this core is the *mantle*, which is thought to be in a kind of plastic state and composed of very dense rocks similar to those found at the surface called *peridotite* (a coarse-grained, dark coloured igneous rock). It may well be that it is movements within this layer that give rise to the earthquakes, volcanoes, and so on that we can observe at the surface of the planet. Lying on top of the mantle is the layer that we have already mentioned, the comparatively rigid crust of the Earth.

It is at the crust that we can see, preserved in the rocks, a record of

the events that have taken place in the Earth's long history as a result of Earth movements and the effects of weather and so on.

Igneous rocks

The crust of the Earth is made of rocks, two-thirds of which are found beneath the world's oceans and seas. If you could stand in a safe place and watch a volcano erupting you would be seeing rocks being formed. The lavas that pour from some active volcanoes are rocks that are so hot (perhaps as much as ten times hotter than boiling water) that they are in a liquid state. These rocks start their life in the mantle of

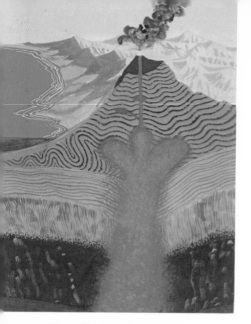

Above: The lava that pours from an erupting volcano is actually rock in a liquid state.
Below: This igneous rock, granite, is formed from (a) quartz, (b) mica, (c) feldspar.

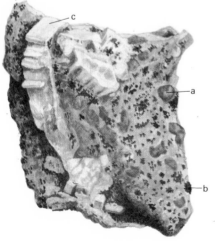

the Earth that has been mentioned earlier. The piece of pumice that you may have in the bathroom is a piece of solidified lava that was once frothy with volcanic gases. Lavas, together with other *igneous rocks* (from *ignis*, Latin meaning fire) such as granite, which form in a different way, are the building blocks of the Earth's skin.

There are many types of igneous rocks and many ways in which they occur. A typical volcanic rock is basalt; the underlying rocks of the oceans are basalts which have poured out from volcanoes along ridges in the centres of the oceanic basins. Surtsey, off Iceland, is a typical volcanic island of this type.

Some igneous rocks, such as the granite that is found on Dartmoor, in Devonshire, England, do not spew out as liquids at the surface, but they cool deep in the Earth's crust so that they have a coarser appearance than the lavas from volcanoes. Igneous rocks are the source from which all the other types of rocks are derived.

Weathering and erosion

Rocks like those we have already mentioned look and feel very hard indeed but they are not indestructible. The action of the weather can destroy rocks. For example, igneous rocks often form in a jointed or cracked manner; water may drip into the joints and in some climates it may freeze. The expansion of water caused by freezing is enough to prise the rocks apart.

In hot desert areas, on the other hand, there is little water to freeze even if it becomes cool enough. Here, however, the wind can have a marked effect on the rocks that have disintegrated, for by carrying the particles of sand and using them like a grindstone it wears away other rocks.

Water is probably the single most important agent of denudation, that is, the wearing away of rocks. Water is a good solvent – it is good at dissolving, particularly when it contains acids from the soil or air. Even granite can be decomposed. Around many granite masses, such as Dartmoor, England, you can see the glistening, white spoil heaps of china clay workings. In such areas, the hard granite has broken down into soft, white clay.

Rain can wear away soft rock or

Rocks may be cracked and shattered by the freezing and thawing of water.

soil, particularly when the resulting mud can be washed away down hill. Some of the rain that falls on the land eventually finds its way into rivers, which are contained in valleys. If you study valleys you will notice that they are usually deep and narrow where the river is in hard rock and is fast flowing, but wide where the river is slower flowing nearer the sea.

Wind-blown sand may form dunes such as those shown below. Pebbles may be shaped by wind-blown sand, too.

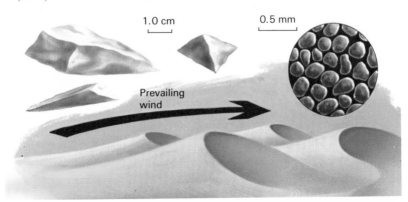

1.0 cm

0.5 mm

Prevailing wind

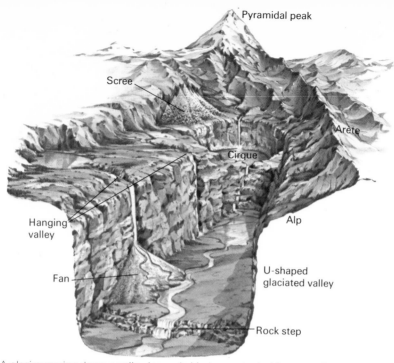

Pyramidal peak

Scree

Arête

Cirque

Hanging valley

Alp

Fan

U-shaped glaciated valley

Rock step

A glacier moving down a valley leaves behind many typical features of erosion after it has melted.

Sometimes you might see that there are quite small rivers in smooth, straight, U-shaped valleys. This is because these valleys were once occupied by frozen water, known as glaciers, which left behind their own special features. Some of these features are shown in the picture above.

Sedimentary and metamorphic rocks

As we have said, the skin or crust of the Earth is made of rocks – in some places covered by water. We shall now look at the way in which geologists classify rocks into three major groups, examine some of the more important rocks, and discuss the fun that can be had just from being a rock hound.

We have already looked at the building blocks of the Earth's crust – the rocks that originate beneath the crust; these are the igneous rocks. There are two other major groups of rocks. The first group, known as *sedimentary rocks*, are, as the name implies, made of the debris from other rocks formed by the processes of denudation, together with other materials such as the broken shells of shell fish and particles that have formed chemically. These rocks may be cemented together, as for example in the typical sedimentary rocks called sandstones, or soft and unconsolidated such as a clay. The individual particles of a sedimentary rock may vary in size from the boulders in a boulder bed to the tiny grains in a clay. The grain size, grain shape, degree of roundness of the grains, composition of the rock, and so on, can indicate the way in which the rock was formed.

The other major group of rocks is referred to as the *metamorphic rocks*. The word, metamorphic, means changed. And so, metamorphic rocks can be derived from any other rocks by the action of heat and/or pressure. They may be formed by the heat around a large igneous body or may occur during major Earth upheavals. A typical metamorphic rock is a gneiss.

Collecting rocks and minerals

We have looked briefly at a few of the many different kinds of rocks. The study of rocks and the minerals that they are made of can be a very complicated business, but you can gain a lot of pleasure from just collecting rocks. A collection can be approached in a haphazard way by just picking up a few pebbles on the beach, or in a way which may lead to a properly organised collection

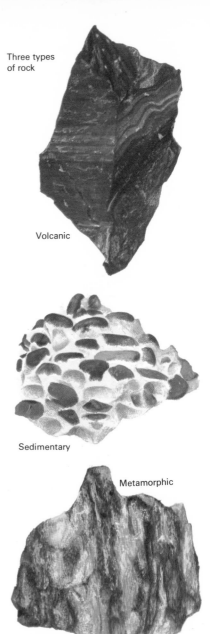

Three types of rock

Volcanic

Sedimentary

Metamorphic

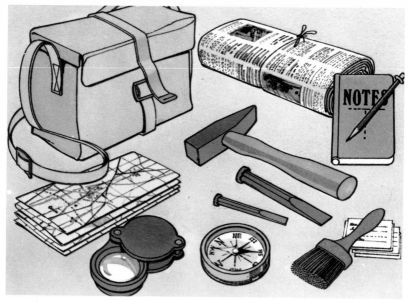

Some of the equipment that is useful for geology field work; the newspaper is for wrapping rocks in.

that you are proud to show your friends. You do not need to be an expert to start with.

Firstly, where are the best places to look for interesting specimens? This depends upon what sort of collection you want to make – many pebbles on the beach are interesting shapes and colours, but they are often hard to identify because they have been worn smooth by the sea. You may wish to collect good examples of igneous, sedimentary, and metamorphic rocks or some of the exciting minerals that may be found. Perhaps the best places to look are quarries, cliffs, and the spoil heaps of mines. But remember, all these places can be very dangerous and you must always ask an experienced person to go with you and get the permission of the owner.

You will need a good map, hammer, hand lens, a note book for entering where and when a specimen was found, paper to wrap rocks in, and a stout bag to carry them home in. A museum will help you identify your rocks.

Fossils and fossil collecting

Imagine what might happen to sea creatures with shells, such as whelks, when they die. Firstly, the soft animal that lived in the shell would decay leaving behind the hard shell. Now, if the conditions were favourable, the shell could be buried in the sediment before it is smashed to pieces. At some later time when the sea has retreated, the sediment may have hardened into a rock with the shell preserved in it. This is how a fossil is formed. A fossil is, in fact, any remains of a once living animal or plant.

Only a very small proportion of living things actually become fossilised and, of course, an even smaller proportion of the soft, fleshy parts of a plant or animal will be preserved. However, it is much more likely that a sea-dwelling creature will be fossilised than any other form of life be-cause fossils are only found in sedimentary rocks, which mainly originate in marine conditions. You are most likely to find fossils in limestone or shale rocks, both of which preserve them well. Fossils are somewhat rarer in coarse sandstones and very rare in pebble beds.

It is perhaps surprising that there are so many fossils until we realise that life has existed on Earth for as long as 3200 million years and during that time many different types of animals and plants have come and gone. Life has only been abundant, however, for about the last 600 million years. In fact, scientists have been able to divide this length of time into different periods on the basis of the animals

The process of fossilization: the live creature; the animal dies and its flesh decomposes; the hard shell is rapidly buried; minerals from the sediments pass into the shell.

age in millions of years	period	era
2	Pleistocene	Caenozoic
10	Pliocene	
25	Miocene	
40	Oligocene	
60	Eocene	
70	Palaeocene	
	Cretaceous	Mesozoic
135	Jurassic	
180	Triassic	
225	Permian	Palaeozoic
270	Carboniferous	
350	Devonian	
400	Silurian	
440	Ordovician	
500	Cambrian	
600	Precambrian	

The illustration shows some of the valuable work undertaken by museums.

Learning about the Earth

and plants living throughout geological time. Unknown rocks can be aged by the presence of certain fossils, and the fossil can also indicate the conditions that prevailed at the time the rock was deposited. Much can also be learned from fossils about the animals and plants themselves.

The same basic techniques may be employed for collecting fossils as was suggested for rocks, but you will only want to look in sedimentary rocks. You need to be very delicate with fossils as a good specimen can easily be destroyed.

Left: The geological column.

If you want to learn about the planet on which you live, you will need a keen eye to observe the world about you and a willingness to learn. Many schools run excellent courses in Earth sciences and you can take examinations in geology and related subjects. Even if you are unable to take part in a formal course, a lot can be learned from visits to museums, and the staff of the Earth science departments of universities and colleges around the world will usually be most helpful. There are many books from which to learn, too, but there is no substitute for experience in the field. Geology is essentially a practical subject and there are still discoveries to be made.

A Guide to the Weather

The droughts in western Europe and the freak weather conditions in other parts of the world in 1976 really proved to us all how much we depend upon the weather. But even in average years, we are affected in many ways by the weather patterns. The weather varies around the world and this is reflected by the plants and animals that live in a given area as well as the food that people eat, the way they dress, the sort of houses they live in, the diseases that are common, and so on. For instance, an Eskimo would not wear a thin, cotton robe and eat fruits and salads any more than a Bedouin tribesman would wear a fur-lined overcoat and eat only rice.

If you want to pursue any outdoor activity, the weather is all important. A game of cricket in England cannot be played in a downpour and winter sports such as skiing cannot take place if it is so warm that the snow melts.

It is always a good idea to check the weather forecast before you set out, if you intend going for a walk in any part of the world where adverse conditions are a possibility. If you go fell-scrambling in the English Lake District, for example, you must take waterproofs and spare clothes with you even though it may be warm when you set out.

The weather is important for any outdoor activity.

Above 480 kilometres (Exosphere)
50% Hydrogen – 50% Helium

IONOSPHERE

Mainly ionised gases

Nitrogen 78%
Oxygen 21%
Argon 0·93%
Carbon dioxide 0·03%
Other gases 0·04%

STRATOSPHERE

Variable amount of water vapour

TROPOSPHERE

The Earth's atmosphere.

The atmosphere

The Earth is surrounded by an envelope of air and water vapour, which we refer to as the atmosphere. The effect that we call weather occurs in the bottom part of this 150-kilometre thick layer of gases. The atmosphere is composed mainly of the gas nitrogen (almost four-fifths) together with oxygen, which makes up the bulk of the remaining fifth. There are also some rarer gases such as argon and xenon, but these need not concern us here. The other two components, water vapour and the gas carbon dioxide, are present in varying amounts. For example, the air in a busy industrial area contains more carbon dioxide than in a sparsely inhabited, densely wooded region. The amount of water vapour present has an important effect on the prevailing weather.

As you probably know, climbers on Mount Everest have to rely on oxygen equipment to breathe. This is because the atmosphere becomes thinner with altitude. The temperature of the atmosphere falls with an increase in height, too. However, it is what goes on at the bottom of the atmosphere that we shall look at.

The 'cause' of weather – the Sun

Energy is needed to make the wind blow and similarly, all the weather processes need energy to drive them.

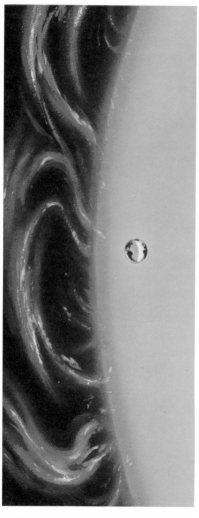

But where does this energy come from? Heat and light are forms of energy and, of course, these are provided by the Sun. The Sun can be thought of as the 'engine' which drives the Earth's processes. All engines need fuel, but in a car engine or even a nuclear engine the fuel has to be constantly replaced, whereas the Sun seems to shine for ever.

Unlike the Earth, the Sun is made up entirely of gas. The energy it provides comes from a process which is called *fusion*. In other words, the tiny particles of which all matter is made, called *atoms*, are continually joining together and as they do so, vast amounts of energy are released. In this case, atoms of the gas hydrogen join together in pairs to form atoms of the gas helium.

The energy from the Sun is given out in the form of radiation, which affects the Earth and its surrounding atmosphere in different ways, depending upon the material through which it is passing. For example, the shiny surface of a calm lake reflects much of the energy and does not become very hot, whereas a building made of dark materials absorbs the energy and warms up quite quickly. You have probably already learned that it is much cooler to wear light coloured clothes in hot weather and now you know why. These variations contribute to the different climates which prevail around the world.

The Sun is enormous when compared to Earth; it is the 'cause' of weather.

The elements of weather

The picture below shows a typical selection of the instruments that may be found at a weather station. These instruments give us an idea of the individual factors that the weather is 'made of'. You can see that there are three types of thermometers for measuring the temperature. One of these is inside a screen so that the Sun cannot shine directly on it; this thermometer measures the true air temperature. On clear nights, the ground temperature may be lower than the air temperature and this may be recorded by the grass minimum thermometer. The third type of thermometer measures the temperature of the soil.

There is a wind vane together with an instrument called an anemometer. These two instruments measure the direction and speed of the wind respectively.

A rain gauge measures the amount of rain that falls in any given period of time and there is a sunshine recorder to give an indication of the number of hours of sunshine in a day.

In addition to all these instruments, a weather station also has a barometer, which measures the air pressure. It is difficult to think of the air having weight but, in fact, at the Earth's surface, a column of air one centimetre by one centimetre by the height of the column (the height is from the surface to the limit of the atmosphere) weighs about a kilogram, depending on the weather conditions.

Some of the instruments that are used at a weather station.

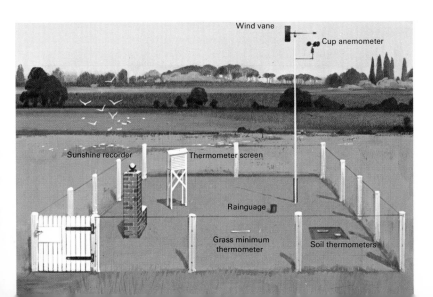

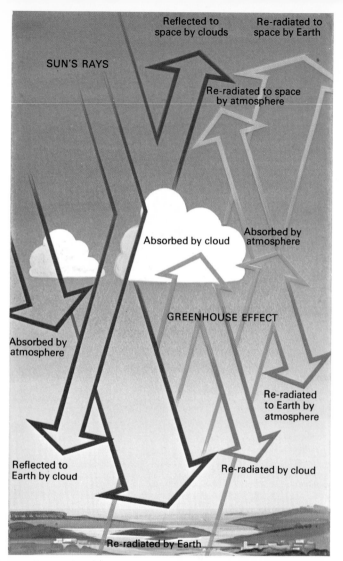

This diagram shows what happens to the energy that arrives at the Earth from the Sun. If the air is free from dust and smoke, it absorbs very little of the Sun's radiation, which passes directly to the Earth's surface, where it is partly absorbed and partly reflected. Some of the outgoing radiation is absorbed by water vapour (or clouds) and reflected back to Earth, thus keeping the Earth's surface warmer than it would otherwise be. This is known as the 'greenhouse effect'. All these variations give rise to the various effects of the weather.

240

Clouds and rain

The rather complicated-looking diagram on page 240 gives an indication of what happens to the rays of sunlight that reach the Earth. Some of the Sun's radiation causes water to evaporate from the oceans and rivers and from growing plants, giving rise to the water vapour that was mentioned earlier. When this water vapour cools, it condenses to form the various types of clouds that you will have seen at one time or another. There are two main types of cloud: cumulus, which results from the cooling of a rising column of air and water vapour, and stratus, which occurs when there is a pocket of cool air between layers of warm air. The drops of water that make up a cloud are so small that they are light enough to float in the air.

Before it can rain, water droplets in a cloud have to join together to form large enough drops to fall; the actual process of raindrop formation is very complicated, however, and is beyond the scope of this book. If the temperature at cloud level is below freezing point and the air temperature beneath this is low enough, the water will freeze and fall as snow or, under certain conditions, particularly during thunderstorms, the water will freeze into small lumps of ice that are called hail stones. Hail stones the size of golf balls have been reported but these are very unusual; a diameter of about 60 millimetres is normal.

Formation of Cumulus cloud

Cumulus

Wind

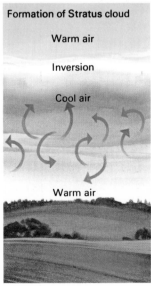

Formation of Stratus cloud

Warm air

Inversion

Cool air

Warm air

The formation of two types of clouds.

Forked lightning occurs during thunderstorms. The lightning momentarily gives rise to great heat and the resulting sudden expansion and contraction of the air sets up sound waves, which are heard as thunder.

Thunder and lightning

One particular weather phenomenon which many people find very frightening are thunderstorms in which lightning flashes across the sky accompanied by loud claps of thunder. It should be remembered that the thunder claps are not caused by clouds banging together as is sometimes thought. If you observe a storm carefully, you will notice that the thunder always follows the flash of lightning. The lightning is like a huge spark caused by an electrical discharge within a thunder cloud. You can imagine that a spark on this grand scale would be very hot and it is the sudden expansion and contraction of the air caused by the heating and cooling effect that produces the bang. When forked lightning is a long way away or is hidden by the cloud, it is seen as a brief flash of light; this is called sheet lightning.

Lightning, like all electricity, tends to be drawn to earth and is attracted by conductors such as a tall tree, so you should never hide under one during a storm – you would be safer in the open.

Weather maps and forecasting

The weather maps that you may see during the weather forecast on television or in the daily newspapers, in the synoptic charts as they are called, look very confusing. They are not quite so complicated as they seem, however. The first thing you might notice are the lines that look like contour lines on an ordnance survey map. These are isobars and they indicate lines of equal air pressure. You will notice that they form shapes like the contours for mountains and valleys. These are areas of high and low pressure, or anticyclones and cyclones. They give an indication of the wind direction because air flows from high to low pressure areas. However, because of the rotation of the Earth, the wind is diverted so that in the northern hemisphere the low pressure is to the left of the wind direction, while in the southern hemisphere it is to the right.

The lines with points or semicircles on them indicate cold fronts and warm fronts, that is, the boundaries between different masses of air. Cold fronts usually give cool, showery weather, whereas warm fronts, bring a wide belt of continuous rain, perhaps followed by finer weather. Sometimes, a warm front and a cold front join together, resulting in what is known as an occluded front. At an occluded front the weather may be rain, followed quickly by a period of clear weather and then showers.

A typical weather chart.

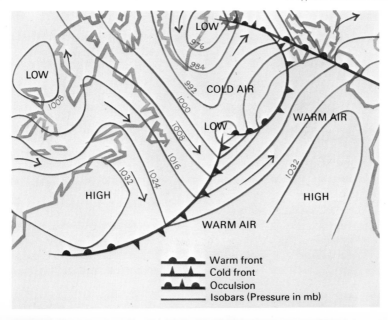

Force	0	1	2	3	4	5
Description	Calm	Light air	Light breeze	Gentle breeze	Moderate	Fresh
Effect						
Weather symbol	◎					

The Beaufort Scale

We have already discussed how important it is to be aware of the weather when undertaking any outdoor activity. Just imagine how important the weather, and in particular, the wind speed, would have been in the days of sailing ships.

The Admiral, Sir Francis Beaufort, who lived from 1774 to 1857, devised a scale of wind speeds that was intended to indicate simply and quickly the effect of wind of any given force on sailing ships and on the sea itself. This scale is still used today but it has been adapted to indicate the effects upon things on dry land. For example, at gale force 1 or light air, a column of smoke would be diverted, but the wind would not be strong enough to cause a change in the direction of a wind vane. On the other hand, a wind of speed gale force 9 or a strong gale would be powerful enough to damage the roof of a house. These terms are commonly used in shipping forecasts.

Watching or listening to the weather forecast is a great help, but it has not always been so easy. In the past, there was no organised weather service and people looked

6	7	8	9	10	11	12
Strong	Moderate gale	Gale	Strong gale	Whole gale	–	–

for signs, many of which have been put into common sayings.

The Beaufort Scale of wind strength indicates the effect of wind of any given force upon things on dry land.

Weather lore

You have probably heard the expression, 'Red sky at night, shepherd's delight; red sky in the morning, shepherd's warning'. This suggests that if there is a red sunset then the following day will bring fine weather, whereas if the dawn is accompanied by a red sky then the day will not be very pleasant. Then there is the saying, 'The north wind doth blow and we shall have snow'. This is not always true, of course, but it does indicate quite correctly that bad weather often accompanies a wind from the north.

If you see a halo around the moon on a clear night this is said to be an infallible sign that there is wet weather to come. Of course, in Britain and Europe, this is very likely to be true because the weather is so variable anyway. In fact, the halo around the moon occurs when there is a certain type of cloud present that often precedes rain.

Further reading list

Map Reading and Navigation

An Introduction to Mapwork and Practical Geography, J. Bygott and D. C. Money (University Tutorial Press)
Map Reading and Interpretation, P. Speak and A. H. C. Carter (Longmans)
Ordnance Survey Maps: A Descriptive Manual, J. B. Harley (Ordnance Survey, Southampton)

Outdoor Safety and Survival

Safety on Mountains, a pocket booklet by John Jackson and other members of staff at the Plas y Brenin National Mountaineering Centre, North Wales (The British Mountaineering Council)
Safety on the Hills, a booklet published by The Scout Association

Book of Survival, Anthony Greenbank (Wolfe Publishing)
Mountain Hypothermia, a booklet by the Safety Committee of the British Mountaineering Council
How to Stay Alive in the Woods (USA), Bradford Angier (Collier Books, New York)
Instant Weather Forecasting, A Watts (Adlard Coles)

First Aid

Modern First Aid, A. S. Playfair (Hamlyn all-colour paperbacks)
First Aid Manual (joint publication of St. John Ambulance Association, St. Andrews Ambulance Association and British Red Cross Society)
First Aid Junior Manual (British Red Cross Society)
New Essential First Aid, A. Ward Gardner and P. J. Roylance (Pan Books)

Walking and Hiking

The Hike Book, Jack Cox (Lutterworth Press; currently being revised)

Publications of H.M.S.O. are especially valuable for walkers in Britain. These include the Forestry Commission Guides, edited by the late H. L. Eldin, and Long Distance Footpath Guides.

Regional Books Series, an extensive series by specialist authors, covering much of Britain (Robert Hale)

The Yorkshire Dales, Marie Hartley and Joan Ingilby (Dent)

Youth Hostels Association – publications produced for its members

Hostelling News, a quarterly tabloid published by the YHA and distributed by post to members

Hillcraft

Mountaineering, Alan Blackshaw (Penguin Books)

Camp and Trek, Jack Cox (Lutterworth Press)

Expedition Guide (Duke of Edinburgh's Award)

The Mountain Code, a booklet by the British Mountaineering Council

Mountain Life, a bi-monthly magazine which is the official journal of the British Mountaineering Council

Orienteering

Discovering Orienteering, Tony Walker (Shire Publications)

Your Way with Map and Compass, John Disley (Blond Educational)

The Silva Compass Instructional Leaflet; one of these is included in the pack with every Silva compass sold

Know the Game Orienteering, J. D. Watson (E. P. Publishing)

Sport Orienteering, Martin Henley (E. P. Publishing)

Orienteering, John Disley (Faber & Faber)

This is Orienteering, Tony Walker and Jim Rand (Pelham Books)

Orienteering for the Young, Peter Palmer (The British Orienteering Federation)

Camping

Modern Camping, Alan Ryalls (David and Charles)

Lightweight Camping (Mobile Camping), Jack Cox (Lutterworth Press)

The Outdoor Cookbook, Jack Cox (Lutterworth Press)

Scout Camping, Tony Kemp and

Jeremy Sutton-Pratt (The Scout Association)

Better Camping, Alan Ryalls and Roger Marchant (Kaye & Ward)

Camp and Trek, Jack Cox (Lutterworth Press)

Sports

General

Complete Book of Sport, Euan and Kate Sutherland (Ward Lock)

Rules of the Game, The Diagram Group (Corgi Books)

Conditioning for Sport, N. Whitehead (E. P. Publishing)

Angling

Freshwater Fishing, Colin Gamble (Hamlyn all-colour paperbacks)

Sea Fishing, Clive Gammon (Hamlyn all-colour paperbacks)

Archery

Beginner's Guide to Archery, Tom Foy (Pelham Books)

Athletics

Athletics for the 70's: A training manual, Ian Ward and Denis Watts (Arthur Barker)

Tackle Athletics This Way, Denis Watts (Stanley Paul)

Canoeing

Canoeing Complete, Brian Skilling (Kaye and Ward)

Cricket

Cricket – How to Become a Champion, John Snow (William Luscombe)

Association Football

Football, Teach Yourself series, F. N. S. Creek (English Universities Press)

Rugby Football

Rugby for Beginners, Ray Williams (Souvenir Press)

Golf

Tackle Golf This Way, John Stobbs (Stanley Paul)

Sailing

Sailing, John Davies (Hamlyn all-colour paperbacks)

Skating

Let's Go Skating, Howard Bass (Stanley Paul)

Skiing

All About Skiing, Mark Heller (Hamlyn)

Swimming

Swimming and Water Sports, Joseph Edmundson (Arthur Barker)

Water Skiing

Master Water Skiing, Gerald Maurois and Maxime Vazeille (Denoel, Paris; Souvenir Press, London)

Horses, Riding and Pony-trekking

Horses and Ponies, Judith Campbell (Hamlyn all-colour paperbacks)

Riding with Elwyn Hartley Edwards (Hamlyn)

Successful Riding and Jumping, Robert Owen (Hamlyn)

My Learn to Ride, Robert Owen (Hamlyn)

Buying and Keeping a Horse or Pony, Robert Owen and John Bullock (Beaver Books)

Caring for a Horse or Pony, Robert Owen and John Bullock (Beaver Books)

Outdoor Hobbies

The Outdoor Book, Jack Cox (Lutterworth Press)

This title contains detailed reading lists for a wide range of outdoor hobbies.

Introducing Geology, D. V. Ager (Faber & Faber)

Canoes and Canoeing, P. W. Blandford (Lutterworth Press)

Guide to the Waterways of the British Isles, (British Canoe Union Handbook)

Making and Flying Kites, Lloyd, Mitchell and Thomas (Beaver Books)

Hamlyn all-colour paperbacks
Many titles including:
Birdwatching, David Saunders

Beachcombing and Beachcraft, Joyce Pope

A Guide to the Seashore, Ray Ingle

Seashells, S. Peter Dance

Teach Yourself
Many titles in this series published by English Universities Press:
Geology, Dr A. Raistrick
Archaeology, S. Graham Brade-Birks
Cycling, R. C. Shaw

Conservation and Nature Spotting

Wild Animals of the British Isles, Dr. Maurice Burton (Frederick Warne)

Tracks, Trails and Signs, Fred Speakman (Bell)

Understanding Ecology, Elizabeth T. Billington (Kaye & Ward)

Butterflies, Robert Goodden (Hamlyn all-colour paperbacks)

Ecology, Michael Allaby (Hamlyn all-colour paperbacks)

The Hamlyn Guide to Birds of Britain and Europe, Bertel Bruun and Arthur Singer (Hamlyn)

Activities for young naturalists, V. E. Graham (Hulton Educational Publications)

Birdwatching, David Saunders (Hamlyn all-colour paperbacks)

A field guide to the Mammals of Britain and Europe, Brink (Collins)

The Hamlyn Guide to the Seashore and Shallow Seas of Britain and Europe, A. C. Campbell (Hamlyn)

Mushrooms and Toadstools in colour, Else and Hans Hvass (Blandford Press)

My World of Nature, Derek Hall (Hamlyn)

Observer Books

This series of pocket handbooks for the identification of all wildlife, trees, wild flowers, fungi, lichens, ferns and grasses (Frederick Warne)

A Guide to the Earth

Rocks, Minerals, and Crystals, D. C. Almond and D. G. A. Whitten (Hamlyn)

The Hamlyn Guide to Minerals, Rocks and Fossils, W. R. Hamilton, A. R. Woolley and A. C. Bishop (Hamlyn)

Fossils and Fossil Collecting, Roger Hamilton (Hamlyn all-colour paperbacks)

Principles of Physical Geology, Arthur Holmes (Thomas Nelson)

British Regional Geology, Institute of Geological Sciences (H.M.S.O., London)

Geology, A. J. Smith (Hamlyn all-colour paperbacks)

The Penguin Dictionary of Geology, D. G. A. Whitten and J. R. V. Brooks (Penguin Reference Series)

A Guide to the Weather

The Weather Guide, A. G. Forsdyke (Hamlyn all-colour paperbacks)

Weather, R. S. Scorer (Phoenix House)

Understanding Weather (Pelican Books)

Metric conversion table

Linear measure	Liquid measure	Avoirdupois weight
1 cm = 0·394 in	1 ml = 0·035 fl oz	1 gram = 0·035 oz
1 m = 3·281 ft	1 litre = 1·760 pint	1 kg = 2·205 lb
1 km = 0·621 mile		

Index

Numbers in bold refer to illustrations.

Useful Addresses

John Bartholomew & Son Ltd, Map Publishers, Duncan Street, Edinburgh, EH9 1TA.

Blacks of Greenock (tents, equipment, outdoor clothing), P.O. Box 6, Port Glasgow, Renfrewshire *and* Ruxley Corner, Sidcup, Kent.

P. W. Blandford (canoe plans and designs), Quinton House, Newbold-on-Stour, Stratford-on-Avon, Warwickshire.

Ellis Brigham (outdoor clothing, camp equipment), 14 Cathedral Yard, Manchester; 73 Bold Street, Liverpool and Capel Curig, North Wales.

British Canoe Union, 26 Park Crescent, London, W1.

British Mountaineering Council, Crawford House, Precinct Centre, Manchester University, Booth Street East, Manchester, M13 9RZ.

British Trust for Ornithology, Beech Grove, Tring, Hertfordshire.

Camping Club Ltd., 11 Lower Grosvenor Place, London, SW1.

Central Council of Physical Recreation, 158 Great Portland Street, London, W1.

Council for the Preservation of Rural England, 4 Hobart Place, London, SW1.

Council for the Preservation of Rural Wales, Y Plas, Machynlleth, Gwynedd, Wales.

Countryside Commission, 1 Cambridge Gate, Regent's Park, London, NW1.

Duke of Edinburgh's Award Office, 2 Old Queen Street, London, SW1.

Forestry Commission, 25 Savile Row, London, W1.

German Camping Club, 8 München 23, Mandistrasse 28, West Germany.

The Girl Guides Association, 17–19 Buckingham Palace Road, London, SW1.

H.M.S.O., P.O. Box 569, London, SE1 9NH and 13A Castle Street, Edinburgh, EH2 3AR.

National Mountaineering Centre, Plas y Brenin, North Wales.

Nature Conservancy, 19 Belgrave Square, London, SW1.

Ordnance Survey, Romsey Road, Maybush, Southampton, SO9 4DH.

Rough Stuff Fellowship (Cycle Campers), 9 Matlock Road, Broadholme, Belper, Derbyshire.

Royal Society for the Preservation of Birds, Sandy, Bedfordshire.

The Scout Association, Baden-Powell House, Queen's Gate, London, SW7 5JS.

World Scout Bureau, Case Postale 78, 1211 Geneva 4, Switzerland.

The Youth Hostels Association, Trevelyan House, St Stephen's Hill, St Alban's, Hertfordshire.

YHA Travel and Services Dept., 29 John Adam Street, WC2.

The Youth Hostels Association (Cycle Hire Scheme), 116 Birmingham Road, Lichfield, Staffordshire, WS14 9BW.